An Introduction
to
Ethical Theories

D1196013

John G. Messerly

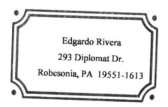

Edgardo Rivera
293 Diplomat Dr.
Robesonia, PA 19551-1613

University Press of America, Inc.
Lanham • New York • London

Copyright © 1995 by
University Press of America,® Inc.
4720 Boston Way
Lanham, Maryland 20706

3 Henrietta Street
London, WC2E 8LU England

All rights reserved
Printed in the United States of America
British Cataloging in Publication Information Available

Library of Congress Cataloging-in-Publication Data

Messerly, John G. (John Gerard).
An introduction to ethical theories / John G. Messerly.
p. cm.
Includes bibliographical references and index.
1. Ethics.
BJ10112.M47 1994 171—dc20 94–23950 CIP

ISBN 0-8191-9823-4 (pbk: alk. paper)

⊖™The paper used in this publication meets the minimum
requirements of American National Standard for information
Sciences—Permanence of Paper for Printed Library Materials,
ANSI Z39.48—1984

For Jane

"...a lily among the thistles..."

Song of Solomon 2:2

Contents

Preface

"We declare at the outset that we do not make any positive assertion that anything we shall say is wholly as we affirm it to be. We merely report accurately on each thing as our impressions of it are at the moment."
Sextus Empiricus

This book grew from my experience teaching philosophical ethics the past eight years. It neither proposes ethical answers nor pronounces moral dogmas. Rather, I try to be equitable, impartial, and unbiased toward each theory as far as is humanly possible. Each theory, I believe, advances the persistent philosophical discourse into the nature of ethical truth. A truth found, I would argue, not in individuals or authorities but in the community of participants in the perpetual dialogue. In the final chapter, I do disclose some of my own insights, but do not claim any privileged moral status for these convictions.

It is my firm belief that philosophical hubris is pernicious, and I find contemptuous and pompous all dogmatic declarations concerning a topic as elaborate and intricate as philosophy. It seems to me that philosophical hubris emanates from two sources: 1) a lack of regard for the complexity of philosophical problems; and 2) an immodesty approaching vanity. Philosophical questions demand humility, reverence--and a touch of humor! Perhaps this is what Bertrand Russell had in mind when he said that philosophy "removes the somewhat arrogant dogmatism of those who have never travelled into the region of liberating doubt."

Furthermore, I assert that more of the world's evil has been caused by a few serious-minded, fanatical, ideologues than by all the skeptics, relativists, and fallibilists combined. Nevertheless, it is easy to be ideological, and I admit falling victim to the disease myself. It is facile, as E.O. Wilson asserted, to measure our "personal emotional responses to various alternatives as though consulting a hidden oracle." I reject this propensity. My emotions and intuitions are not crystal balls, but products of a prolonged process of evolutionary change.

However, philosophers tend toward the adoption of fervent and impassioned doctrines because, unlike scientists, philosophers do not have to go around "digging for the facts." Most philosophers have no idea of how difficult it is to tease out from reality even the smallest bit of truth, and they can say almost anything they like without being reprimanded! Both professional and amateur philosophers, as well as ordinary individuals, are susceptible to this misguided conceit.

If the enigmatic questions of philosophy are not amenable to trite and effortless solutions, then an intellectual quest is the appropriate response to our bewilderment. The search requires arduous and painstaking toil, but returns immense and lasting reward. This is why I believe the search for truth is greater than the mere affirmation of it. Walt Whitman exhorts us to make this journey:

I have no chair, no church, no philosophy,
I lead no man to a dinner-table, library, exchange,
But each man and each woman of you I lead upon a knoll,
My left hand hooking you round the waist
My right hand pointing to landscapes of continents and the public road.

Not I, not any one else can travel that road for you,
You must travel it for yourself.

Acknowledgements

When I was a graduate student at St. Louis University, three individuals played momentous roles in my life, career, and education. Theodore R. Vitali brought wisdom, humor, and justice to his position as chair of the philosophy department. His efforts on my behalf will never be forgotten. William C. Charron single-handedly taught me to write by spending untold hours pouring over my work. I have tried to emulate, without success, his precision of intellect and dignity of character. Richard J. Blackwell directed my dissertation and conducted the most inspiring seminars of my graduate career. I am both proud and humbled to have been his apprentice, and he remains for me, as he has been for generations of students, an archetype of wisdom. Each of these individuals displays continuing interest in my life and career. For their assistance, advice, encouragement, knowledge, friendship, and wisdom...I remain forever indebted.

But my philosophical education began before exposure to professional philosophy. As a young boy, countless hours spent with my father, Benjamin Edward Messerly, kindled my philosophical curiosity. Though he had little formal education, my father possessed a sharp and probing mind and was a philosopher until the end. I hope he would be proud. And without the assistance of my mother, Mary Jane Hurley Messerly, the education I so cherish would never have been attained. For every hour I gave to my studies, she spent one with my children. She serves as a constant reminder not to let a part of the heart get lost in the learning. Fate has been extraordinarily kind to me.

I would also like to thank my children: John Benjamin, Katie Jane, and Anne Marie. They have encouraged me, motivated me, and endured their father's countless hours in his "closest" study. They are special; each and every one. Anne wants to learn to read and when she does, new worlds will appear. Our searches are the same; we both want to be more than we are now. Katie checked the chapter headings and typed a few of the electric blips that became this book. She was always asking, "Dad, how's your book going?" She has a heart full of warmth and a mind full of questions. John programmed the computer to say: "Dad, I love you and don't forget to give me a copy of your book!" That message helped keep me going. He also played a special role in extricating me from a number of technological conundrums associated with this computer technology. Without his "trouble-shooting," many hours would have been unproductive. Children are...life renewing itself.

My colleague at Ursuline College, Dee Christie, carefully and conscientiously read large portions of this manuscript. She provided thoughtful comments, criticisms, and suggestions. I thank her for clearing up a number of difficulties and ambiguities surrounding my interpretation of natural law theory and for her support and encouragement throughout the entire project.

I owe the greatest debt--one which cannot be adequately repaid--to Laurence Mazzeno, Vice President for Academic Affairs and Academic Dean at Ursuline College. Dean Mazzeno read the entire manuscript and offered perceptive and insightful comments, criticisms, and suggestions. During the process, I came to appreciate and respect the depth and breadth of his historical, literary, and philosophical knowledge. Furthermore, he gave countless hours of his own time to the numerous and endless details of producing this text. He was, simultaneously: reader, editor, motivator, consultant, agent, philosopher, and friend! It would simply have been impossible to complete the manuscript on time and in present form without him. I also found myself reinvigorated both by the process and his encouragement. I was launched. If indeed my purpose is "to sail beyond the sunset, and the baths of all the western stars," then it was he who blew the wind when my sails stood still. Where would we be...anyone...without the winds that blow us?

Finally, I would like to thank my wife Jane for never losing faith in me through all these difficult years. Shared struggle creates a bond unbreakable by sorrow and misfortune. Unity sustains us and is the wellspring from which emerges new hope, new life, and new love. May it be that way always. In my life I have known heartache and anguish, but knowing Jane, I know a little of what life and love may be...

Chapter 1

What is Philosophy?

"The nations wax, the nations wane away; In a brief space the generations pass. And like to runners hand the lamp of life one unto another."
  Lucretius

1. The Beginnings of Rationalistic Thinking

The word **philosophy** comes from two Greek roots meaning "the love of wisdom," and a philosopher is thus "a lover of wisdom." In the Western world, philosophy traces its beginnings to the ancient Ionian city of Miletus, the richest city in the ancient Greek world. There, on the eastern edge of the Mediterranean in the sixth century B.C.E., the Greeks systematically applied human reason to questions concerning nature and human life *without* reference to the supernatural.

For example, Thales (c.585 B.C.E.), the father of Western philosophy, advanced an explanation--that the earth is made of water--which could be discussed in a rational forum. His successors subsequently rejected his argument, arguing instead that physical reality is composed of the bound-less (Anaximander), air (Anaximenes), fire (Heraclitus), the four elements (Empedocles), or an infinite number of seeds (Anaxagoras). Both monism--the view that one kind of thing composes reality--and pluralism--that many stuffs compose reality--encountered difficulties. Monism could not account for plurality and pluralism could not account for unity.

Greek thinking about the nature of the physical world culminated with Democritus (460-360 B.C.E.), who argued that all of reality was made up of empty space and tiny, solid, indestructible *atoms*. This theory provided a theoretical solution to "the problem of the one and the many," by pos-tulating a qualitative singularity and a quantitative plurality. Material things were identical regarding the qualitative nature of the atomic "stuff" but differed in the number and configuration of the atoms.

This theory also resolved the "problem of change," the paradox of how something can change into something else and yet remain the same. How are you now *both* the same person and a different person from when you were a small child? If you are the same, you are not different. And if you are different, you are not the same. Heraclitus (c.500 B.C.E.) proposed that everything was constantly changing, whereas Parmenides (c.515-450 B.C.E.) asserted that permanence was the fundamental reality and used Zeno's famous arguments against the possibility of motion to support his views.

Zeno argued that the swift Achilles could never pass a front-running tortoise in a race because, by the time Achilles reached the place where the tortoise was previously, the tortoise had moved on to some further place along the race course. When Achilles reached that point, the tortoise had moved on again. This repeated itself infinitely, so that Achilles could never pass the tortoise. Because we ordinarily assume motion is possible, the atomists and other pluralists rejected Parmenides and Zeno.

The Atomists argued that atomic transformations account for our perception of change. In reality, the number and configuration of atoms change, but their underlying qualities do not. What we perceive as change is in fact quantitative transformation at the atomic level. In little more than a century, rational discourse without benefit of experimentation had ad-vanced the argument remarkably.

But atomic theory was not the only achievement of Greek rationalism. Alexander the Great spread Greek influence throughout the Mediterranean and, over the next several centuries, the accomplishments of rationalistic thinking were impressive. Hipparchus mapped the constellations and calculated the brightness of stars. Euclid produced the first systematic geometry. Herophilus argued that the brain was the foundation of intelligence, and Heron invented gear trains and steam engines. Eratosthenes calculated the circumference of the earth with amazing accuracy, mapped the earth, and argued that the Indies could be reached by sailing west. (Yes, ancient scholars knew the earth was round!) This brief synopsis does not even mention Pythagoras the mathematician, Archimedes the mechanical genius, Ptolemy the astronomer, or Hippocritus the physician.

In Alexandria, where over the course of seven centuries the rationalistic spirit flourished, the great library and museum held the knowledge of the ancient world. But this rationalistic spirit never seized the imagination of the masses and, in 415 A.D., the mob came to burn down the library. At that time, the greatest mathematician, scientist, and philosopher at work in the library was *Hypatia*.

Unfortunately, Alexandria in Hypatia's time was in disarray. Roman civilization was in decline and the Catholic Church was growing in power. Cyril, archbishop of Alexandria, despised Hypatia because of her friendship with the Roman governor and her place as a symbol of rationalism and paganism. On her way to work in 415 A.D., she was met by a fanatical mob of Cyril's parishioners. "They dragged her from her chariot, tore off her clothes, and, armed with abalone shells, flayed her flesh from her bones. Her remains were burned, her works obliterated, her name forgotten. Cyril was made a saint."

Though the pursuit of knowledge continued in the Middle East and in Eastern civilization, Western civilization would soon plunge into the dark ages and await the Renaissance, more than a millennium in the distant future, for the rebirth of the rationalistic spirit which began in ancient Greece. We can only speculate as to the increased extent of our scientific knowledge today had the spirit of this investigation continued unabated.

2. Philosophy's Domain

So far we have made no distinction between rational, philosophical, and scientific thinking because the ancient Greeks did not. When Thales or Democritus practiced what we might call physics or chemistry, these disciplines were still *a part of* philosophy. As the centuries proceeded and various parts of philosophy became more successful and specialized, the sciences formed their own distinct disciplines. However, this is a relatively recent phenomenon. Newton, for example, considered his revolutionary seventeenth-century work in physics to be in the field of *natural philosophy*. The natural sciences as distinct disciplines are thus relatively recent, and the social sciences even more so. Economics became an independent discipline in the nineteenth century, psychology in the late nineteenth and early twentieth centuries, and sociology in the 1930s.

Today, in the colleges and universities of the Western world, the residual, unanswered, and timeless questions which do not fall within the specific purview of other disciplines comprise most of philosophy's domain. Therefore some of the most difficult questions, for which there are *as yet* no definite answers or methodology, remain for philosophers to consider. For example: Is the belief in God reasonable? What is knowledge? Do we know anything for certain? What is the ultimate nature of reality? Why is there something rather than nothing? What is the nature of goodness, beauty, truth, liberty, equality, and justice? What is a good political system or fair economic system? What is valuable in art, music, or human conduct? What is morality? Are human beings free? What is the meaning of science? What is the relationship between thought and reality? What is language? Are human beings entirely material, or do they have a spiritual nature as well? What is the meaning and purpose of human existence? These are just a sample of philosophical questions.

Most of these questions fall into a few basic groups. **Metaphysics** probes the nature of ultimate reality and revolves around the question, "what is real?" **Epistemology** studies the nature and limits of human knowledge and centers on the question, "what can we know?" **Axiology** explores the nature of the valuable in art, politics, and ethics and asks, "what is good?" Since philosophy invokes reasoned arguments to support positions--rather than faith, authority, tradition, or conventions--**logic** is that branch of philosophy that differentiates good arguments from bad ones.

In addition, many specialized fields exist within philosophy's domain. For instance, we may legitimately speak of a philosophy of religion, mathematics, science, law, medicine, business, language, or even sport. Note, one can *practice* any of these without philosophizing about them. You can be cleric, mathematician, scientist, lawyer, nurse, physician, business executive, linguist, or athlete *without* philosophizing about that which you practice. Thus, philosophy is by nature a theoretical pursuit rather than a practical one. Philosophers ask: how do we know a religious claim is true? Does mathematics tell us about reality or is it merely an arbitrary formal system? How do we know scientific theories are true? What justifies the use of legal coercion? What should the practice of medicine entail? Are ethical behaviors and profitable business compatible? Does language effectively communicate ideas? What purpose do sports serve? Any important part of human culture, the culture as a whole, or the ultimate nature of reality itself is ripe for analysis. Thus, *philosophy is sustained, rational, and systematic reflection and analysis of the philosophical area in question.*

In addition philosophers investigate the relationship between, for example, philosophy and psychology, literature, art, culture, gender, and history. Can one do philosophy independent of these forces or does one's philosophy depend on them? Some philosophers study the history of philosophy to understand the evolution of ideas in history; others do philosophy of history in an attempt to determine the meaning of human history. Philosophers are interested in theoretical issues in game theory, decision theory, and cognitive science, as well as practical issues concerning business, medical, and environmental ethics. Thus, the range of philosophy is enormous.

For the uninitiated to get a grasp of the nature of philosophy, they should go into any library or bookstore and examine a work of non-fiction. Often, at the end of the work in question, one finds a section entitled "Afterthoughts," "Reflections," "Postscript," "Epilogue," "What It All Means," etc. At that point, the authors no longer write about physics, psychology, or history but reflect on the *meaning* or *implications* of their investigation. At that point, they are philosophizing.

3. Philosophy, Science, and Religion

In order to more clearly conceptualize philosophy's territory, one must consider it in relationship to two other powerful cultural forces with which it is intertwined: *religion* and *science*. We may characterize the contrast between philosophy and religion as follows: *philosophy relies on reason and experience for truth; religion depends on faith, authority, and revelation for truth.* Of course, any philosophical position probably contains some element of faith, inasmuch as reasoning rarely gives conclusive proof; and religious beliefs almost always contain some rational support, since few religious persons rely completely on faith.

The problem of the demarcation between the two is made even more difficult by the fact that different philosophies and religions--and even philosophers and religious persons within similar traditions--place dissimilar emphasis on the role of rational argument. For example, Eastern religions traditionally place less emphasis on the role of rational arguments than do Western ones, and in the east philosophy and religion are virtually indistinguishable. In addition, individuals in a given tradition--like Roman Catholicism for instance--differ in the emphasis they place on the relative importance of reason and faith. So the difference between philosophy and religion is one of emphasis and degree. In general, *religion is that part of the human experience whose beliefs and practices rely on faith, grace, authority, or revelation to a significant degree.* Philosophy gives little, if any, place to these parts of human experience. Religion stresses faith and trust, philosophy reason and doubt.

Distinguishing philosophy from science is equally difficult because many of the questions vital to philosophers--like the cause and origin of the universe or a conception of human nature--increasingly have been taken over by cosmologists, astrophysicists, and biologists. Some formulate the distinction in terms of methodology, the scope of the disciplines, or their ability to arrive at ultimate meaning. But difficulties exist with all these proposed distinctions.

Regarding meaning, many scientists derive existential meaning and metaphysical beliefs from their scientific theories. Concerning scope, contemporary "Theories of Everything" purport to explain the origin and nature of everything. Perhaps methodology best distinguishes the two, since philosophy relies on argument and analysis rather than empirical observation and experiment. In this way, philosophy resembles theoretical mathematics more than the natural sciences. Still, philosophers utilize evidence derived from the sciences to reformulate their theories. Remember also that, until the nineteenth century, virtually every prominent philosopher in the history of western civilization was either a scientist or mathematician. In general, we contend that *science explores areas where a generally acceptable body of information and methodology directs research involved with unanswered scientific questions.* Philosophers explore philosophical questions *without* a generally acceptable body of information.

Philosophical analysis ponders the future relationship between these domains. Since the seventeenth-century scientific revolution, science has increasingly expropriated territory once the exclusive province of both philosophy and religion. Will the relentless march of science continue to fill the gaps in human knowledge, leaving less room for the poetic, the mystical, the religious, and the philosophical? Will religion and philosophy be archaic, antiquated, obsolete, and outdated? Or will there always be questions of meaning and purposes that can never be grasped by science? Betrand Russell (1872-1970), one of the twentieth-century's greatest philosophers, elucidated the relationship between these three domains:

> All *definite* knowledge--so I should contend--belongs to science; all *dogma* as to what surpasses definite knowledge belongs to theology. But between theology and science there is a [Nobody's] Land, exposed to attack from both sides; this [Nobody's] Land is philosophy.

4. The Value of Philosophy

What is the value of philosophy? To this question we propose some possible answers. First, it is *natural* to wonder, to ask questions. Children are marvelous philosophers who never tire of asking questions. However, you may reply that nature does not necessitate duty and that you do not find it natural. Second, we claim that philosophizing is *pleasurable*. We find great joy asking questions and considering possibilities. Perhaps that is why Plato called philosophizing "that dear delight." Nonetheless, you might counter that it does not suit your tastes. Third, we appeal to philosophy's *usefulness*. Any kind of knowledge is at least potentially useful, and if philosophy engenders not merely knowledge but wisdom, its worth appears definite. Nonetheless, you may not value either wisdom or knowledge unless it engenders material reward.

Finally, we argue that philosophy *defends* against unsupported ideology, unjustified authority, unfounded beliefs, baseless propaganda, and questionable cultural values. These forces may manipulate us if we do not understand them and cannot think critically about them. This does not require a *rejection* of cultural values, only a reflection upon them. Otherwise, they are not *our* values, ideals, or beliefs--we have simply accepted them second-hand. To this you might respond that reflection is laborious, that ignorance is bliss, and that trust in authority and tradition maintain the continuity of culture.

Therefore, you could conceivably reject all of our arguments. In the absence of definitive arguments, individuals must decide whether philosophy is a worthwhile pursuit. We all decide, in our own lives, whether the pursuit of wisdom, knowledge, wealth, fame, pleasure, or anything else is worth the effort. In the end, to value philosophy we must *believe* that reflection, questioning, contemplation, and wonder *enrich* human life; we must believe, with Socrates, that *"the unexamined life is not worth living."*

Questions about the value of philosophy entwine with issues concerning education. What is the point of education? Is it merely to learn practical techniques? Consider a nurse or physician who has mastered all of the techniques necessary to practice their professions. Are they *complete* nurses or physicians? Most of us would say no; they need to understand the persons they treat holistically, and this knowledge does not come merely from their technical training. Thus, we do recognize the place in our education for philosophy, literature, poetry, and history even though they may not be *practical*. However, if material needs are all that matter to practical persons, then the life of the mind will be irrelevant for them.

Imagine instead, that education increases our awareness, diminishes our dogmatism, and enables us to be capable of happiness and wisdom. Is the point of lifting weights merely to push them against the force exerted by gravity? No! We seek instead to transform our physiques, accomplish our goals, learn the valuable lesson that nothing comes without effort, and that life's greatest joys accompany personal struggle and subsequent triumph. And through this process we are literally *transformed!* Analogously, education transforms us in an even more fundamental way. Jiddu Krishnamurti (1895-1986) stated the case as follows:

> Why do we go through the struggle to be educated? Is it merely in order to pass some examinations and get a job? Or is it the function of education to prepare us while we are young to understand the whole process of life? Surely, life is not merely a job, an occupation: life is wide and profound, it is a great mystery, a vast realm in which we function as human beings.

In this context, Russell contended:

> The [person] who has no tincture of philosophy goes through life imprisoned in the prejudices derived from common sense, from the habitual beliefs of

[their] age or [their] nation, and from convictions which have grown up in [their] mind without the cooperation or consent of [their] deliberate reason. To such a [person] the world tends to become definite, finite, obvious; common objects rouse no questions, and unfamiliar possibilities are contemptuously rejected. As soon as we begin to philosophize, on the contrary, we find...that even the most everyday things lead to problems to which only very incomplete answers can be given. Philosophy....removes the somewhat arrogant dogmatism of those who have never travelled into the region of liberating doubt...

Finally, consider the view of the great twentieth-century historian and philosopher Will Durant on the purpose of philosophy:

> Philosophy will not fatten our purses...For what if we should fatten our purses, or rise to high office, and yet all the while remain ignorantly naive, coarsely unfurnished in the mind, brutal in behavior, unstable in character, chaotic in desire, and blindly miserable?
>
> Our culture is superficial today, and our knowledge dangerous, because we are rich in mechanisms and poor in purposes... We move about the earth with unprecedented speed, but we do not know, and have not thought, where we are going, or whether we shall find any happiness there for our harassed souls. We are being destroyed by our knowledge, which has made us drunk with our power. And we shall not be saved without wisdom.

5. What is Philosophical Ethics?

Ethics is that part of philosophy which deals with the good and bad or right and wrong in human conduct. It asks: What is the good? What should I do? What is a good life? Is morality objective or subjective? Is it absolute or relative? Why should I be moral? What is the relationship between self-interest and morality? Where does morality come from? What, if anything, provides the ultimate justification for morality? Should one emphasize duty, happiness, or pleasure in moral judgments? Like all philosophical questions, these are not amenable to easy solutions.

Traditionally, ethicists sought to give general advice on how to live a good and happy life, and almost all of the most influential ancient, medieval, and even some of the modern philosophers construed their task this way. Contemporary philosophers have increasingly moved to more abstract and theoretical questions. While some contemporary philosophers have voiced alarm at this trend, and suggest reinvestigating traditional ethical approaches, many contemporary ethicists still ask esoteric questions.

We may conveniently divide contemporary philosophical ethics into at least four distinct parts. **Meta-ethics** conducts an analysis of moral concepts, ethical justification, and the meaning of moral language. **Descriptive ethics** describes ethical behavior among various people and in various cultures. (Social scientists now do most of this work.) **Normative** ethics contemplates the norms, standards, or criteria that serve as theories or principles for ethical behavior. **Applied** ethics applies normative theories to particular ethical problems. These problems include moral issues in law, business, medicine, nursing, population control, science, sexuality, or the environment, just to name a few.

This book deals with a few meta-ethical issues, but it is primarily a treatise on normative theory. These normative moral theories delineate particular norms, standards, or criteria for moral conduct and try to answer two basic questions. First, *what is the nature of morality?* And second, *why should I be moral?* Consequently, this book examines a few of philosophy's timeless questions.

6. Morality, Manners, and Law

Morality is often confused with other areas of human activity and experience. For example, morality is not the same as manners, since manners are essentially a matter of personal or cultural convention. There are overlaps between the two areas, but we can see that they are not the same. For instance, we display bad manners if we constantly blow our nose on our shirt, but we would not call this action immoral.

It is especially important to differentiate morality and law, inasmuch as discussion of the moral and legal often conflate. On the one hand, the two differ since we believe some legal acts to be immoral and some laws to be unjust. And normally even if legal regulations did not prohibit murder, stealing, and the like, it is likely we would still consider them wrong. This suggests that the two are not coextensive. On the other hand, the two are connected because the law embodies many moral precepts. Legal prohibitions incorporate most of our ordinary moral rules such as those against lying, killing, cheating, raping, and stealing. This suggests there is a connection between the moral and legal.

Though it is possible to have morality without law or law without morality, the two usually go together. Therefore, we suggest that *law codifies morality*. In other words, the law formulates the culture's morality into legal codes. Again, not every legal code refers to a moral issue, but most laws do have some moral import. Though a connection between the moral and legal exists, they are not the same thing.

While a thing's illegality may give us a reason not to do the thing, this is a prudential rather than moral reason. In other words, if we are afraid to steal because we might get caught, then we fear punishment, not immorality. Nevertheless, we might offer moral reasons to abide by the law. We could say that we owe it to the state to abide by their laws and that civil disobedience undermines both the moral fabric and our tacit agreement with the state. This was essentially Socrates' argument against escaping from Athens before his impending execution. But in general, legal arguments are not applicable to ethical discussion. Ethicists do not discuss a thing's legality, they discuss a thing's morality. Thus, we may discuss the moral independent of the legal, since the mere fact that something is illegal does not mean it is immoral.

7. Moral Theories and Intuitions

The moral theories we encounter in this book often conflict with our moral intuitions. In other words, attempts to explain the nature of morality perplex many of us because the proposed explanations are sometimes *counter-intuitive*. Explanations, theories, or beliefs are counter-intuitive if they violate our ordinary, common-sense view. For example, it is counter-intuitive to suppose that physical reality is illusory, although there is no way to demonstrate this is not the case. Similarly, it is counter-intuitive to suppose the keyboard upon which I type is moving, even though the keyboard, room, earth, solar system, galaxy, and entire universe move! This demonstrates that our non-moral intuitions are often mistaken.

Certainly our moral intuitions are sometimes wrong too. To illustrate this point, consider some moral beliefs once thought to be consistent with our ordinary moral intuitions: the doctrine of natural slavery, the inferiority of women, the acceptability of human sacrifice, severe corporeal punishment, debtor's prisons, dueling, and witch burning, just to name a few. Since most of us now believe these practices are wrong, we must admit our former moral intuitions were mistaken. But have we really cleared up the matter? Is it not possible that many of our present moral intuitions will, at some later time, be rejected? For instance, can we not imagine that at some future time meat-eating may be thought barbaric? And if we reject a present intuition at some later date, then they are not sacrosanct now.

Therefore, the mere fact that a theory violates our moral intuitions is not necessarily a reason to reject the theory; we might reject our intuitions instead. How do we resolve the dispute between the two? One of the ways of resolving the dispute between moral intuitions and moral theories is to achieve what many contemporary philosophers call *reflective equilibrium*. Reflective equilibrium calls for a balance or equilibrium between moral intuitions and theories. If a theory radically contradicts our moral intuitions, then the theory should probably be rejected. If, on the other hand, the theory has a number of explanatory and justificatory advantages and only slightly challenges our moral intuitions, then the intuition should probably be rejected. This is one way of dealing with the conflict.

But most classic moral theories are not counter-intuitive. In fact, they are classic because they explain so much of our ordinary moral consciousness. Nonetheless, since no theory is perfect, almost any proposed moral theory generates some counter-intuitive results. Perhaps this reveals to each of us, that we do not have a *privileged moral status*. If our moral status were privileged, then we could measure any proposed theory against it. But throughout this book, we will assume that our moral status and intuitions are not privileged. They do not provide unique insight into moral truth. If our moral status were privileged this investigation would be irrelevant, since we would already possess moral truth. During the course of the book, we assume that a theory *might* be rejected because it is counter-intuitive, but the fact that a theory is counter-intuitive *does not* definitely refute it.

The same issue applies when we turn from explaining morality to justifying it. Contemporary philosophers offer three basic kinds of justification for morality. Some, following Plato, argue that morality is based in self-interest. Others, following Hume, suggest that morality rests upon some sentiments, emotions, or sympathies we happen to have. Others, following Kant, insist that morality is grounded in reason. In addition to these philosophical justifications, some metaphysicians and theologians maintain that the source of morality rests in the metaphysical order. Whatever our moral intuitions about moral justification, we assume that these intuitions are not privileged.

8. Moral Theory and Practice

Just what is the relationship between moral theory and practice? Ideally, a well-considered theoretical framework would be implemented in a moral life. Unfortunately, this is not always the case. We can easily imagine both an unethical ethics professor and an ethical maintenance worker. In fact, we know of no studies which support the view that ethics professors are more ethical than maintenance workers or that college students who take ethics courses are more ethical than those who do not. It could be that there is no relationship between moral theory and practical results.

On the other hand, we know of no studies that support the opposite view and no evidence that suggests we benefit by ceasing moral theorizing. It is always hoped that theory will have some implications for practice. Much here revolves around the issue of what moral theorizing will uncover. It may uncover no good reasons for ethical conduct, in which case we might give up morality. It could also give us reasons to be moral of which previously we were unaware. But whatever our inquiry uncovered, we still must make ethical choices. At the very least, the inquiry informs that choice.

9. A Word about Methodology

This book *objectively investigates*, as far as it is humanly possible, various ethical theories pointing out their strengths and weaknesses. This method may persuade us that there are no ethical truths; that philosophical ethics is *nothing but* opinions. Of course this could be true, but moral relativism, like any position, must itself be scrutinized. The mere fact that the method treats all theories as equal candidates for moral truth, does not mean that they are equal. Easily confused is the assumption that "there are two sides to every story" with the conclusion that "both sides are equally true."

Thus, the method should not determine our beliefs about moral truths, and it is easy to see why this is the case. Suppose the book's method assumed that Kant's theory was the *only* valid moral theory, in other words, that there was only "one side to every story." In that case, the book's purpose would be to push Kant's theory at the expense of all others. That book would not educate; *it would indoctrinate*. And, if we uncritically accepted Kant's theory, it would not be our own. Therefore, if we do not want dogma, then we should not allow the method to determine our beliefs.

Still it can be tedious, examining the arguments for and against various positions. With this in mind, let me share a story. When a young undergraduate philosophy student first encountered St. Anselm's ontological argument for the existence of God, he was completely convinced that the proof, so long sought, had been found. But the subsequent presentation of Gaunilo's reply to Anselm left him devastated; the argument did not work. Later, an analysis of Anselm's reply to Gaunilo fortified his previous belief in the validity of the argument. Later still, the doubt returned and the student eventually rejected the argument. Now you might say that a careful, meticulous, conscientious, and painstaking analysis is laborious. And, *you are right!* But in the process of this intellectual journey, the student was transformed. On this point, listen to how Benedict de Spinoza, the inspiring seventeenth-century Dutch lens-grinder, ended his famous ethical treatise.

> It [peace of the soul] must indeed be difficult since it is so seldom discovered, for if salvation lay ready to hand and could be discovered without great labor, how could it be possible that it should be neglected by almost everybody? But all noble things are as difficult as they are rare.

Of course, we all want to be comfortable in our beliefs. But how do we decide what to believe? Charles S. Pierce, a famous nineteenth-century American philosopher, was particularly interested in the epistemology of belief. How do we and how should we determine our beliefs? Pierce believed that rational analysis, instead of authority or tradition, should determine them. But why then do so few persons do this? Because, he said, belief is a tranquil state, and we like to persist in believing precisely what we now believe. Perhaps this explains why questioning our beliefs is so difficult. Whatever the reasons we cling to our beliefs, the intellectual journey demands that we question our assumptions and subject them to careful scrutiny. But it does not demand that we reject them. We might come to understand them! Exhorting us to embark upon this intellectual quest was T.S. Eliot:

We shall not seek from exploration
And the end of all our exploring
Will be to arrive where we started
And know the place for the first time.

Chapter 2

Impediments to Ethical Theory

"I do not know how to teach philosophy without becoming a disturber of the peace." Benedict De Spinoza

1. Nihilism

The word nihilism derives from the Latin *nihil* meaning "nothing" and refers variously to: 1) the denial of any basis of knowledge; 2) the general rejection of conventional morality or religion; 3) the doctrine that social progress can be achieved only by the destruction of social and political organizations; or 4) the general belief that life is without meaning or purpose. **Ethical nihilism** denies the validity of all moral distinctions; thus, helping an elderly woman cross the street does not differ *morally* from stealing her purse! To put it more bluntly, the nihilist finds nothing wrong with *killing your mother*!

Ethical nihilism is a *counter-intuitive* moral theory. As we saw before, a doctrine is counter-intuitive if it offers a fundamental challenge to any strongly held moral intuition (belief). For example, if I claimed that a deity rewards the wicked and punishes the virtuous, you would likely reject the doctrine as counter-intuitive. Analogously, we reject ethical nihilism--which finds nothing wrong with killing your mother--because it opposes our ordinary moral intuitions.

Thus, ethical nihilism denies the possibility of an enterprise woven within the fabric of human intellectual history and of the utmost practical importance. If killing your mother for your inheritance does not differ morally from calling her on Mother's Day, then the entire moral enterprise is obviously immaterial. Fortunately, most of us do not believe this.

2. Determinism

Determinism takes many forms: physical, psychological, biological, historical, social, economic, etc. In any of its formulations *determinism affirms that all facts in the universe, including facts about human choices, are conditioned by and dependent upon prior causes*. Thus, the doctrine is indistinguishable from fatalism, the view that what will be must be. For our purposes, the most important implication of determinism is that prior causes determine the human will, and, therefore, humans are *not* morally responsible for their behavior since *they are not free*.

If the doctrine is true, then why ask, "what should we do?" Prior causes determine what we do, and these causes were themselves produced by other causes *ad infinitum*. We easily see how the chain of causality can be traced backward to some state of affairs outside of our control. For example, we have no control over our genetic inheritance or social environment. So when we say that we *ought* to do something, we are unable to do so be-cause our behavior has been determined. According to the determinist, we *cannot* change our behavior. But, if we cannot do something, it makes no sense to tell us that we ought to do it. Ethicists have often expressed this idea by saying "ought must imply can."

To understand the theory, ponder the following case. You stand by an open window with a small child in your arms. Suddenly, some maniac appears from behind, tears the child from your arms, and hurls it out the window to its untimely death. Certainly, no one would hold *you* responsible for the child's death. Contrast this case with one in which you are by the window again, but this time the child's crying agitates you. As your anger builds, you suddenly throw the child out the window. Here it seems *you* are responsible. But wait! In both cases something *caused* the child's death. In the first case, clearly the maniac did. But what about the second? What caused you to throw the child in that case? Was it your agitated state? And if so, what caused you to be easily angered by a child's cry? Your high stress level? Your biochemistry? The beatings you endured when you were young? Surely you are not responsible for the myriad of causes, whether physiological or environmental, that make you particularly susceptible to a child's cry! If previous causes regulate human choices then *free will is illusory.*

A vehement defender of environmental determinism in the twentieth century was the Harvard psychologist B.F. Skinner. In his ground breaking work *Beyond Freedom and Dignity* (1971), he argued that we should move beyond the notions of freedom and dignity and admit that the environment determines human behavior. Essentially, according to Skinner, we need to create an environment that rewards--positively reinforces--the kinds of behavior we encourage and punishes--negatively reinforces--the kinds of behavior we forbid.

Another kind of determinism--genetic determinism--has surfaced in the last twenty years largely through the work of Harvard scientist E.O. Wilson's important books *Sociobiology* (1975) and *On Human Nature* (1978). Wilson argues that all human social behaviors, including ethical ones, are reducible to biology. Evolutionary advantages wired into the DNA determine human behavior. Again, no matter what form determinism takes, its central claim is that our notions of human freedom are archaic and implausible.

In the course of this brief essay, we cannot enter into the complicated debate concerning freedom and determinism. But we can say that much contemporary evidence supports determinism and that modern science presupposes a connection between cause and effect. Immanuel Kant (1724-1804), one of the greatest of modern philosophers, considered cause and effect to be one of the most fundamental presuppositions of science, without which science was not possible. Most of us are familiar with the basic idea. Pavlov's dogs, for example, have been conditioned to salivate when they hear a bell. And genetic make-up determines many character-istics like intelligence, physical stature, eye and hair color. We also hear about evidence that links certain behavioral tendencies like homosexuality or alcoholism to genetic influence. Rational thinking would not be possible without this connection between cause and effect.

But remember an important point. Science has *not* demonstrated that a particular genetic make-up completely *determines* behavior. The current scientific view states that a proclivity, propensity, inclination, or tendency toward a kind of behavior *may have genetic influence*. But that is not the same as saying that genes determine behavior. Similarly, while humans respond to various forms of environmental conditioning, it has never been demonstrated that they are *completely* determined by them. Thus, most thinkers today opt for some form of *soft determinism* as opposed to the *hard determinism* we have been discussing. Soft determinism, as opposed to hard determinism, posits the compatibility of free will and determinism.

However, there exists another reason to reject determinism. *It has largely been abandoned by modern physics!* In the early part of this century, physics discovered that nature, at the sub-atomic level, is not strictly deterministic. In fact, *indeterminism* operates in this realm. Put simply, the present does not exactly determine the future at the sub-atomic level, and so we may say that the universe at its most basic level exhibits freedom. According to the majority of physicists, this indeterminacy does not result from our inability to measure the sub-atomic realm more precisely, but is built into the fabric of reality.

We might also reject determinism because it is counter-intuitive. We have a strong intuition that we choose freely and that, for example, we could stop reading this paragraph if we wanted to. Finally, why should we believe the determinists anyway, since the construction of their theory was merely determined!

3. Skepticism

Skepticism holds that knowledge is, if not impossible, almost impossible and refers also to a general attitude of doubt or disbelief toward any positive assertion. Thus, skepticism is an epistemological position which asserts that human knowledge is, if not impossible, at least uncertain. What we call the *weak version* of **moral skepticism** claims that moral knowledge--even if it exists--cannot be known to be true. Contrast this with the *strong version* of moral skepticism which declares that *there is no objective moral knowledge.*

The weak version involves debatable epistemological claims about the nature of human knowledge. It affirms that some "truth" about morality may exist, but such knowledge is beyond human comprehension. In defense of this view, one might point to the fact that moral judgments have been mistaken in the past, thereby severing the connection between our judgments and the truth about a matter. But how does a skeptic know past moral judgments were mistaken? Consistent skeptics must be skeptical of their own judgments. How do *they* know, as skeptics, that moral knowledge is impossible? Are they absolutely certain? If they are, then they have contradicted themselves.

Such considerations have led some philosophers to adopt a related view known as *fallibalism,* the conviction that any idea we have about the world *might* be wrong. In other words, some beliefs and ideas we have about reality are probably correct, but their truth cannot be *absolutely* ascertained. However, this uncertainty should not undermine the moral enterprise. The strong version of moral skepticism presents a stronger challenge to morality and must defend the thesis that objective moral knowledge is imaginary. We now turn to some of these arguments.

4. Relativism

When we say the true, good, or beautiful is **relative**, we contrast it with **absolute**. If you say the beauty of the painting is relative or "in the eye of the beholder," you affirm that there is no absolute truth about whether it is, in fact, beautiful or not. If an art authority stands in the rain for hours waiting to see the recent work of a famous artist while you do the same to see your friend's doodling, *as a relativist*, the authority cannot say that you do not know art because "it's all relative." If you eat healthy, exercise regularly, maintain an ideal weight, and see a physician periodically, while your roommate eats compulsively, lives a sedentary life, gains weight, and does not have physical check-ups, you cannot *as a relativist*, argue that you live healthier because "it's all relative." If you have a Ph.D. in Physics from Cambridge University and have recently advanced a "unified field theory," while your best friend believes she is a poached egg and that the world is made up of tiny "gremlins," you cannot, *as a relativist*, claim that you are any more likely to be correct about the nature of physical reality than she is.

On the face of it, such a view seems preposterous. Is it really true that nurses do not know more about nursing than farmers? Or that farmers know no more about farming than nurses? Physicians are no better at medicine than auto mechanics and vice versa? You might object. Those are areas about which there can be definite knowledge so they are *not* relative; but there is no definite knowledge about morality, religion, and poetry. But if morality is relative, what is it relative to?

5. Cultural Relativism

It is often claimed that morality is relative to, conditioned by, or dependent upon **culture**. In support of this claim, individuals often point to the differences between the moral codes of various cultures. Since cultures have different moral codes, they argue, *there is no objective truth about morality*. Of course, the relativity of morality does not follow merely from cultural differences. If cultures disagree about the acceptability of human sacrifice, for example, that doesn't show that there is no truth about whether the practice is moral. *It might be that one of them is acting immorally!* Thus moral disagreement, by itself, does not establish relativism.

Some cultural mores--funeral practices or gender relationships--are relative to culture, but all cultures share some basic values. For example, they all protect their young, prescribe truth-telling, and discourage gratuitous violence. Without such values, they would not survive. Of course, the mere fact that there are some universally shared moral codes does not conclusively prove that morality is absolute. *The cultures might all be wrong!* Thus, moral agreement, by itself, does not establish absolutism.

Nonetheless, cultural relativism produces some counter-intuitive results. For instance, we could never judge other cultures by any absolute standard, inasmuch as no such standard would exist. We could not condemn societies that tortured all persons over fifty or banished bald persons to Siberia because the culture defines moral truth. We would have to condone Nazi extermination of Jews, since no objective standard would allow condemnation. Correspondingly, the idea of moral progress would make no sense. While we may admit *some* relativity of morality across cultures, we certainly reject the view that *all* of morality is relative.

6. Personal Relativism

If we follow the implications of cultural relativism to their logical conclusion, we are led to a new theory that morality is relative to **personal** beliefs, opinions, attitudes, feelings, emotions, desires, wants, inclinations, tastes or preferences. In this theory, moral judgments and moral truths are relative to, dependent upon, or conditioned by, persons or subjects. (This theory is also referred to as *subjectivism*.) Here are a few ways of expressing the basic idea.

1. You have your opinion and I have mine and that's the end of it.
2. Morality is about feelings, not facts.
3. Values are subjective, not objective.
4. My moral beliefs cannot be wrong, since they are based on my feelings and emotions.

However we formulate the theory, its message is clear. Moral disagreements revolve around opinions, tastes, and preferences. Disagreements about the morality of abortion or homosexuality are similar to disagreements about spinach! Some people like spinach and some do not. But there is no point in trying to change people's minds about spinach because we all have different tastes. Hence, according to the subjectivist, when we assert "x is wrong," we are really only reporting our dislike or disapproval of x, and when we say "x is right," we merely voice our approval.

But are disagreements about the morality of slavery, for instance, just like those about spinach? Of course, if you really believe slavery is wrong you do disapprove of it, but is that all there is to it--your disapproval? If that is the case why do people discuss, argue, and fight about moral disagreements but not about disagreements over spinach? (Except possibly with your mother!) Don't both sides in the disagreement assume they are *right* and that the other is *wrong*? Don't they assume that some objective standard of morality exists? Furthermore, if you say "an individual has a right to enslave others," and I say "an individual has no such right," the relativist says we are *both* right! But this is clearly contradictory.

Finally, suppose I tell you that *I like to torture small children in the most painful way possible.* Surely there is something wrong with that, but a relativist must accept my actions, since moral truth depends on me and I like to torture them! This is so implausible, that morality cannot be *exclusively* a matter of personal opinions, feelings, tastes, preferences, etc.

7. Emotivism

The argument *for* personal relativism has been advanced in the twentieth century by the American philosopher Charles Stevenson (1908-1979). Stevenson brought linguistic analysis to the aid of his relativistic theory to produce a more radical relativism called *emotivism*. In essence, this theory states that moral judgments *express* personal **emotions**. Consider any declarative statement like:

"Abe Lincoln was the sixteenth president of the United States."
"The St. Louis Cardinals won the World Series in 1964."
"The Earth is larger than the sun."

These statements, like all declarative statements, are *either* true or false. They state facts, whether true or false ones, but they do not simply express emotions. Command statements, "Get out!" or "Shut the door!" for example, are *neither* true or false. Now think about the following:

"Go Cleveland Browns!"
"All right!"
"Hurray for the army!"

It is easy to see that these statements are *neither* true or false; they merely express our emotions. In the language of contemporary ethics, they do not have cognitive content; they are *non-cognitive.*

Now what about moral statements? If you say "Gandhi was a good man," or "homosexuality is evil," are you expressing your emotions or making a factual assertion? Emotivists believe the former. If you say "homosexuality is evil," this equals, so the emotivists contend, the expression "homosexuality, yeech!" In other words, while the statement appears to have cognitive content, in reality I merely express my revulsion toward the practice. Analogously, if I say "homosexuality is good," this equals "homosexuality, all right!" Similarly, "Gandhi was a good man" equals "yeah Gandhi," and "Gandhi was a bad man" equals "boo Gandhi." This returns us full circle to our earlier discussion of relativism. When art experts prefer famous paintings to my doodling, they say, in essence, "yeah, famous art!" But there is no difference between famous art and my doodling, so the emotivist maintains, except in the emotions one has toward them.

The emotivist also claims that moral judgments serve another purpose; we use them to persuade others. The statement "x is wrong" tries to persuade others not to do "x". Presumably, this strategy succeeds more often than merely expressing our emotions. But couldn't there be another reason why we try to persuade others that "x" is wrong? And couldn't that reason be because x really is wrong? If you say "Gandhi was a good man" don't you believe that he possessed some qualities, virtues, or character traits that we all recognize as objectively good? Otherwise, we have no retort to individuals who claim that Hitler was a good man, since *they* feel good about *him*. And when we point out that Gandhi read, studied, and practiced Hindu philosophy, was a spiritual and disciplined man who regularly meditated and fasted, and who gave his life for his countryman, Hitler devotees will simply acknowledge your emotions toward Gandhi and express theirs toward Hitler.

So we are at impasse. On the one hand, the statement, "Gandhi was a good man," is not factual in the same way as are declarative sentences. On the other hand, it does not strictly express emotions either. It has been suggested, by both classical and contemporary philosophers, that a third alternative presents itself: *moral truths are truths of reason.* Perhaps we have already given good reasons why Gandhi was a good man and can give good reasons why Hitler was not. We can point to Hitler's masterminding the extermination of millions of people or to his action as a catalyst for world war. The moral truth would depend upon where the weight of reason lies.

But even this strategy is not decisive. The emotivist may argue that what counts as a good reason for us--that Gandhi meditated--is not a good reason for them. In fact, they could claim that reasons *depend* upon emotions. We like meditation; thus we call it good. Much here depends upon our assessment of the ability of human reason to arrive at moral truth. Needless to say, some philosophers are more optimistic about this than others.

Still, we may *have* given good reasons why Gandhi was a good man or Hitler a bad one, and *others just won't accept them.* Perhaps they are unreasonable! For instance, suppose you ask your professor why you failed the test and the professor responds: "because you have red hair." You might point out that this is not a good reason, inasmuch as hair color should be irrelevant to test scores. If the professor will not listen, it might *not* be because you don't have a good reason, but because your professor won't accept it. We can think of plenty of examples when we provide overwhelming evidence that does not effect recalcitrant individuals.

Finally, we appeal once again to the notion of counter-intuition. If ethics revolves exclusively around feelings, emotions, attitudes, tastes, preferences, interests, wants, desires, and opinions, then there is nothing wrong with torturing small children. Such a theory must be mistaken.

8. Psychological Egoism

Psychological egoism, a kind of soft determinism, maintains that self-interest motivates *all* human action. This is the case *even when it appears that others' interests motivate us.* Reflect upon the individual who robs banks and kills possible witnesses. What motivates the killing? Obviously, the belief that eliminating the witnesses is in the robber's interests. Now what about Mother Theresa who aids the poor of Calcutta? Are her motivations any different? She must believe that helping the poor is in *her* interest because it will make her happy, make her soul more pure, help her get to heaven, or perhaps all three. Therefore, according to the doctrine, non-self-interested action--which exemplifies morality--*is not possible.*

On the surface, the theory seems plausible. We want to join the Peace Corps because we think that's in our interest, whereas our friends want to be drug dealers because they think that's in their interest. And there is some truth to the theory. Mother Theresa, Peace Corps volunteers, and drug dealers all do what they want. But if that's all the theory claims, then it is hardly earth shattering. But it declares much more; it claims that people *always* do what they want because their psychological wiring makes such behavior inevitable. But what argument do its advocates advance to support their claim that people always do what they want? They point to the fact that people do things. The problem with this argument is that it does not show that people always do what they want. Just because people do things does not mean they want to do them.

In fact, people often do *what they don't want to do*. For example, suppose I make an appointment to meet you in my office tomorrow but in the meantime encounter a much more pleasant offer. Say my friends have recently returned from Europe, where they have made a fortune in the philosophy business, and want to "wine and dine" me all day. If I still keep my appointment, I am doing what I don't want to do. Of course, you can say that I didn't want to feel guilty or thought I might lose my job, but couldn't I maintain that I simply thought it was the right thing to do? Certainly, we sometimes do what we don't want to do.

Another problem with the theory revolves around the distinction between self-interest and selfishness. If the theory maintains that we are always selfish--what we will call the *strong* version of psychological egoism--it is obviously mistaken. Mother Theresa and Peace Corps volunteers are not selfish, since they act in other person's interests--the very definition of un-selfishness. If the theory holds that we are always self-interested--what we call the *weak* version of psychological egoism--then it fails as well. As we have already pointed out, all action is not self-interested, if that means doing what you want. In addition, we often act in non-self-interested ways. We smoke cigarettes. We overeat. We do not cultivate our minds. Un-limited examples of non-self-interested behaviors exist. So all actions are not self-interested. We might object that persons, though they do not always act in their interest, are *motivated* by self-interest. For example, the horrors of withdrawal motivate the smoker's actions. But this claim hardly stands up to scrutiny. How is the smoker, the addict, the slothful, or the lazy motivated by self-interest? Aren't they just *self-destructive*?

Thus, the theory contains a trivial truth; people usually do what they want. But the theory, which purports to reduce all human motivation to self-interest, is mistaken. Even if Mother Theresa is *partly* motivated by her own interest, she also wants to do what she believes is the right thing. Therefore, though self-interest powerfully motivates human behavior, it does not motivate it exclusively. Despite psychological egoism's initial plausibility, we conclude that individuals act from a variety of motives besides self-interest.

9. Ethical Egoism

While psychological egoism declares that we always *do* act in our own interest, **ethical egoism** claims we always *ought* to act in our own interest. It *prescribes* certain courses of action as morally obligatory. In contrast to all of the theories discussed so far, it suggests an objective basis to morality. *Moral actions are self-interest actions, and individuals should be moral because it benefits them.* This moral principle applies even if others will be hurt. If it is in my interest to steal your money and I can get away with it, then I ought to do it. However, it does not necessarily imply that I hurt others or act immorally. I may refrain from stealing your money if there is a police officer next to you or if you are armed and dangerous! If I am in a situation where morality and self-interest coincide, then I appear moral. If I am in a situation in which they conflict, then I act immorally. Thus, I act self-interestedly, whatever this entails.

It is exceedingly difficult--as Plato, Locke, Kant, Mill, and others can attest--to refute this theory. In the first place, the egoist may advance the following powerful argument. If we all pursue our self-interest the "cream will rise to the top," which will ultimately benefit us all. This was the classic argument of the economist and philosopher Adam Smith (1723-1790) who, in his masterpiece *The Wealth of Nations*, argued that the release of individual self-interest promotes the economic interests of all. Moreover, the defenders of egoism suggest that some promoters of altruism simply want to live off of the successful; they want our pity and our help. But why reward or encourage those who will not be self-reliant? Why not challenge them to be virtuous and industrious instead? Egoists argue that Altruists reward vice and penalize virtue. This argument has some merit, but is flawed because it really refutes altruism rather than supports egoism. So that even if altruism is misguided, it doesn't follow that we should be egoists.

There are many replies to the egoist. We might say they are blatantly immoral, but why? We may maintain they will not go to heaven or will suffer from a guilty conscience. But they might not believe in heaven or experience guilt. A better strategy would be to point to the danger of a world made up exclusively of egoists. Here, the egoist has two defenses. First, egoists may honestly believe they can prosper in this chaotic world by defeating their opponents; and second, an enlightened egoist may advocate morality, hide their egoism, and prosper against the naive. *They practice, but do not advocate, their egoism.* Finally, you might ask them: "how would you like it if others took advantage of you?" This is a complicated claim. Egoists agree they don't want others to be egoists because that wouldn't be in *their* interest. But why shouldn't they act egoistically? What do they care about *another person's* interests? How do others' interests give them a reason to do anything?

Here we have entered into one of the most difficult disputes in contemporary philosophy. If others' interests give you a reason to act, then this refutes egoism. If, on the other hand, only your interests give you a reason to act, then egoism is irrefutable. Some distinguished contemporary philosophers--for example, Alan Gewirth, of the University of Chicago, and Stephen Darwall, of the University of Michigan--argue the former position while others--like Gilbert Harman, of Princeton University, and Kai Nielsen, of the University of Calgary--argue the latter. Whatever position we take, contemporary ethical theories must respond to egoism. The problem of egoism has become particularly acute in the modern Western world since the rise of individualism in the eighteenth century. The emphasis on individual freedoms, rights, and privileges has lessened our concern for the community.

There is another problem with egoism which deserves closer investigation. It perplexes us that egoists should never publicly advocate their position. *They don't want others to be egoists!* But isn't this inconsistent? What does it mean to defend a theory which you cannot publicly advocate? The contemporary philosopher Jesse Kalin defends egoism against the inconsistency charge. The egoist can consistently maintain, Kalin argues, that others *ought* to act in their own interest but that doesn't mean the egoist *wants* them to. He gives the example of a chess game. I believe that you ought to move and put me in check but that doesn't mean I want you to. Therefore, there is nothing inconsistent about egoism. Others reply that egoism blurs the distinction between the moral and non-moral uses of "ought," and it advocates a strange ethical system. Strange because the egoist must maintain that you really *ought* to knock them (the egoist) down and take their (the egoist's) wallet, but they (the egoist) sure *hope* you (the other) don't. Needless to say, this is a very unusual way of thinking about "ought," since ordinarily when we say someone *ought* to do something we imply that we *want* them to. Another contemporary philosopher, Brian

Medlin, puts the point this way. Is it reasonable to say: "Of course you should do this, but for goodness sake don't?"

Medlin's attack on ethical egoism is controversial, and no argument probably convinces the egoist. When egoists ask why they shouldn't act immorally, perhaps our best reply is simply: "because someone might get hurt." If this response fails to convince them; no others will likely succeed.

10. Hedonism

Hedonism is the doctrine that the only intrinsic good is *pleasure*, and the only intrinsic evil is *pain*. The more pleasure and the less pain an action produces, the more intrinsically valuable it is. In its classic formulation, there are no differences in the *qualities* of pleasures produced by an action; there are only differences in the *quantity* of pleasure. This means that for one individual, eating ice cream is more pleasurable than reading Shake-speare, while for another the reverse is true. According to the doctrine, *you ought to choose that activity, from the choices available, which produces the greatest quantity of pleasure; or, if all available choices are painful, the one with the least quantity of pain.*

According to the hedonist, given the choice between two actions both of which produce pleasure, you ought to choose the one productive of the most pleasure. Given the choice of two actions both of which produce pain, you ought to choose the one productive of the least pain. Given the choice between two actions, one productive of pain the other of pleasure, you ought to choose the pleasurable activity.

We might think of hedonism as a kind of egoism. If egoism claims that you ought to do what is in your own self-interest, hedonism tells you what is in your self-interest--much pleasure and little pain. Immediately, we should ask another question: "Just which life supplies the most pleasure?" The initial response would seem to be a life filled with sensual pleasures--food, drink, sex, and psychological stimulation. Unfortunately, sensual pleasures are often accompanied by physical pain. If one eats too much, indigestion and obesity may follow. If one drinks too much, nausea and headaches may ensue. If one has frequent sexual encounters, all forms of sexual disease may result. And if one takes hallucinogenic drugs, an entire lifetime may be ruined. How many of the rich and famous have come to re-gret following this doctrine. Thus, maximizing pleasure may be self-destructive.

Possibly the most devastating critique of hedonism was offered by Plato in his dialogue the *Gorgias*. Plato asks Gorgias, a hedonist, if scratching an itch is pleasant, and Gorgias agrees that scratching an itch is a pleasant experience. But if pleasure is the only good, Plato argues, then a life spent itching and scratching would be a good life. Gorgias clearly discerns that this is not so, and that pleasure cannot be the only good. Thus, even if pleasure is good, it does not follow that it is the only good or that we should maximize it.

A less radical hedonism was advanced by the ancient Greek philosopher Epicurus, who claimed we ought to seek "mild" pleasures, that is, pleasures not accompanied by pain. For instance, we ought to eat, drink, and have sex, but in a moderate fashion. In addition, we should cultivate the desire for the more refined pleasures of a single glass of wine or the nuances of Eliot's poetry. The problem is that such cultivated tastes take years to acquire and entail sacrifice and temperance along the way. For all the virtues of such a doctrine, it barely resembles our initial version of hedonism. In the final analysis, hedonism is either self-destructive or not specific enough to guide us in determining what we ought to do.

Having overcome the major impediments to ethical theory, let us now turn to the theories themselves.

Chapter 3

Natural Law Ethics

"To disparage the dictate of reason is equivalent to condemning the command of God."
St. Thomas Aquinas

1. The Divine Command Theory

Let us now consider the view that morality rests upon religion. Assuming that a relationship between God and morality exists, how do we characterize it? A classic formulation of this relationship is the **divine command theory** which states that "morally right" means commanded by God and "morally wrong" means forbidden by God.

Philosophically, this theory presents a number of immediate difficulties. Its defense necessitates philosophical arguments to prove God's existence, or at least God's rational plausibility. Next, one needs to determine God's commands. This would be especially difficult, since individuals have postulated many antithetical things as commanded by God including: celibacy and polygamy, the right of kings and social revolt, war and peace,

33

humanitarian aid and witch-burning. But even if one knew God's commands, one would still have *to interpret them.*

This last point presents grave difficulties. Take a simple command, "thou shalt not kill!" When does it apply? In self-defense? In war? Always? To whom does it apply? To animals? Intelligent aliens? Serial killers? All living things? The unborn? The brain-dead? Religious com-mands such as "do not kill," "honor thy parents," or "do not commit adultery" do not manifest the specificity necessary to eliminate the need for human interpretation. Where do the Christian Scriptures speak unequivocally about abortion, for instance? For the sake of argument, let us grant that we can demonstrate God's existence, know God's commands, and interpret them correctly. May we then suppose the divine command theory adequately accounts for morality?

The great Greek philosopher *Plato* suggested that it did not. In the dialogue the *Euthyphro* Socrates posed one of the most famous questions in the history of philosophy: *Is something right because the Gods command it, or do the Gods command it because it is right?* It seems the relationship between God and morality must be characterized in one of these two ways.

If we characterized the relationship the first way, then right and wrong *depend* on God's will. Something is right *because God says so*! Two basic problems attach to this view. First, it makes God's will arbitrary! God could have commanded lying, killing, cheating, and stealing to be right! You might be tempted to say that God wouldn't command us to do these things. But why not? Remember God's will determines right and wrong, on this view, so that if God said, "thou shalt kill," that would be right. The second problem is that the theory renders the notion of God's goodness superfluous. We ordinarily attach meaning to the notion that "God's commands are good." We believe we are attributing a property--goodness--to God's commands. But on this account good simply means "commanded by God" so that "God's commands are good" really just means God's commands are commanded by God," a useless tautology. The basic point is this. Why call God good for issuing arbitrary commands?

If we characterize the relationship the second way, then we must accept some standard of morality *independent* of God's will. In God's infinite wisdom, God knows that truthfulness, for example, is better than untruthfulness. On this view, God commands things *because they are right*. But this is much different from *making* something right. On this second view,

God recognizes or sees the moral truth but cannot change it. Here, God cannot make killing, lying, cheating, and stealing right anymore than we can. Thus, the moral law limits God, since God cannot change it by fiat. If we accept this second option, we have given up the divine command theory.

Two alternatives present themselves if the standard of morality is independent of God. First, the standard may lie beyond our comprehension, forcing us to rely on authority, revelation, or tradition to explain morality. This ends philosophical ethics. The other alternative utilizes human reason to understand God's law. We will now pursue this second alternative.

2. The History of Natural Law Ethics

The genesis of natural law ethics is in the writings of the Greek philosopher *Aristotle* (384-322 B.C.E.), who first identified the natural with the good. All things "aim at some good," he says at the beginning of his most famous treatise on ethics, "and for this reason the good has rightly been declared that at which all things aim." For individuals, ethics is a study of the good, goal, end, or purpose of human life, which is *happiness*. Politics, on the other hand, is a study of the good, goal, end, or purpose of society, which is *human flourishing*.

But what is good? Aristotle distinguished between *real goods* and *apparent goods*. Real goods satisfy natural needs and are good for us *independent* of our desires. Food, clothing, and shelter are real goods because we need them. Apparent goods satisfy acquired wants and are called good *because* we desire them. Shrimp, designer clothes, and mansions are apparent goods; we call them good because we want them. A good life consists in the acquisition, over the course one's lifetime, of all the real (natural) goods. These include external and bodily goods such as food, clothing, shelter, health, vitality, and vigor, and, in addition, "goods of the soul" like love, friendship, knowledge, courage, justice, honor, and skill. To obtain real goods requires that we act with good habits or *virtues*. We must mold our character, the sum total of our habitual actions, so that we consistently pursue the good and moral life. The person of good character exhibits moral virtues such as temperance, courage, and justice, and intellectual virtues like wisdom and prudence. Thus, a life full of virtue is a good one, and, at the same time, it is a happy life, since it fulfills our natural needs and tendencies. Essentially, through the moral life we actualize our unique human nature.

The idea that each thing has as its goal or purpose activity in accordance with its nature, Aristotle called **teleology**. (From the Greek *telos*; meaning goal, end, or purpose.) We can understand this easily if we consider an artifact like a pen. A pen that writes well is a good pen, since it fulfills its purpose. While we give artifacts their purpose, teleology is an intrinsic component of the natural world. Acorns develop into oak trees, caterpillars into butterflies, and little children into mature adults; the eyes are meant to see, the hands to grasp, and the kidneys to purify. We call fulfilled, whatever satisfies its teleology, and we call defective, whatever fails to do so. To be fulfilled means to actualize the potential inherent in the thing, whereas to be defective refers to the failure to do so. Thus, *actualization of natural potential is the essence of teleology and supplies the moral imperative for human beings.*

The *Stoics* further developed the doctrine and first used the term **natural law**. Stoicism flourished in Athens in the third century B.C.E. and later in the Roman Empire in such great figures as Seneca, Epictetus, Marcus Aurelius, and Cicero. Unlike Aristotle, the Stoics believed that human happiness was possible *without* external and bodily goods. They also emphasized rationality and the control of emotions. The Stoics insisted that we have a *duty* to follow nature, particularly our rational nature, rather than convention. The source of natural law was *Logos,* the universal power or energy personified in nature's laws.

That natural laws should prevail over cultural conventions led the Stoics to the idea of the cosmopolitan individual or citizen of the world. Roman jurisprudence, which needed to formulate rules to deal with various cultures, adopted the idea of a natural law for all the world's citizens. Its basic premise was the natural law's independence from cultural mores.

This idea had tremendous repercussions throughout human history and would inform the interaction of western Europe and much of the new world. In the sixteenth century, for instance, the Spaniards vehemently debated its applicability for the civilizations they discovered in the New World, and in the eighteenth century the idea influenced the founders of the American government. But the next great development in the idea after Stoicism occurred in the thirteenth century.

3. St. Thomas Aquinas

St. Thomas Aquinas (1225-1274) synthesized Aristotelianism, Stoicism, and Christianity to give the natural law its classic formulation. In addition to Aristotle's natural virtues he added the *theological virtues*--faith, hope, and charity--and to earthly happiness he added eternal beatitude. For Thomas, action in accordance with human nature fulfills God's eternal plan and Scripture's commandments; thus, *the natural law is God's law known to human reason.* Unlike the lower animals, we have the ability to understand the laws of our nature and the *free will* to follow or disregard these laws. But how do we attain knowledge of the natural law? It is not innate, intuited, or easily derived from sense experience. Instead, we use **reason** to determine the conformity of moral conduct and nature. Since fulfilling natural needs makes us happy, **the natural is the good.** What then constitutes the law? While all mature individuals know its most general principles--like do not kill the innocent--controversy surrounds reasoned conclusions about its specific applications.

The fundamental principle of natural law ethics is *that good should be done and evil avoided.* This general principle may be specified into moral axioms like: "Do not kill!" "Be faithful!" "Preserve your life!" "Care for you children!" "Do not lie or steal!" "Life is a universal human good!" All of these are both natural and good. We further specify these axioms by rational analysis and by reliance on Church, scripture, or revelation. As Aristotle pointed out, natural inclinations and tendencies are good and we fulfill them by acquiring the elements which constitute human happiness-- *the universal human goods*--among which are life, procreation, friendship, and knowledge. Nevertheless, within the boundaries set by human nature, the specific way one satisfies natural inclinations may differ, and thus, a range of activities might satisfy, for instance, our aesthetic or intellectual needs. However, we all need the universal human goods. Thus, morality demands that we follow the laws of our nature which *are the same* for all on the basis of our shared humanity.

Still, we need not satisfy all of our natural tendencies. For instance, we must curb aggression and dishonesty, so that friendship and human society thrive. In this way, we see how *reason* makes value judgments and imposes moral obligations upon us. The moral law demands that we develop our reason and act in accordance with reason's imperatives. As we have seen, nature directs us to live well, flourish in human communities, and, finally, experience the beatific vision. Therefore, beginning with human nature and using reason to determine the goals nature sets for us, we determine what we *ought to do*.

Perhaps a simple illustration may help. If we want to become nurses, then we *ought* to go to college and study nursing. Employing our rational faculties, we impose a non-moral obligation upon ourselves, given an antecedent goal or purpose. Analogously, reason imposes *moral* obligations upon us. If we want friends and friendship demands justice, then we ought to be just. Of course, the examples are very different. Moral obligations may not depend upon self-interest in the same way that non-moral obligations do. But the basic idea is the same, without goals nothing is obligatory. If we don't want to be nurses or don't want friends, then we probably have no obligation to study nursing or be just. And if there are no ultimate purposes in human life, then there probably are no moral obligations either. On the other hand, according to the natural law, the complete actualization of human potential demands, among other things, that we develop our talents and be just. If we fail to do this, we violate the natural law.

4. Double Effect

A fundamental principle of natural law theory is that *human life is an incommensurable good*. Even if good consequences result, we are prohibited from *intentionally* killing the innocent because of the unique and incommensurable value of human life. This emphasis on the intention of a moral action allows us to distinguish between externally similar actions and leads to one of the most important principles in contemporary natural law theory: **the principle of double effect.**

The principle of double effect applies in situations where a course of action will produce *both* good and bad effects. Morality clearly outlaws willing evil acts, either as an end or as a means to an end, but some well-intentioned actions produce *unintended* evil consequences. In such cases, the action is moral *if and only if* it satisfies *all* of the following criteria.

1. The act itself must not be evil.

2. The evil must not be the means to the good. (The ends do not justify the means.)

3. The evil must not be intended. (The good effect only must be intended; the bad effect must be unintended.)

4. There must be a proportionately good reason for permitting the evil.

To illustrate the principle consider the following. A soldier jumps on a hand grenade to save his/her comrades. In this case

1. The jumping by itself is not evil.

2. The evil effect--the soldier's death--is *not* the means of achieving the good effect--saving his/her comrades lives. (Shielding them from the grenade saves their lives.)

3. The soldier does not intend evil--his/her own death. (S/he intends to save his/her comrades.)

4. The soldier has a proportionate reason to save their lives; they are of incommensurable valuable.

Compare this with suicide. If we kill ourselves by jumping on a hand grenade the bad effect--our death--*is* the means of achieving good effect--saving us from being, for example, depressed. When we kill ourselves we also *intend* our death and our depression is *not* sufficient reason to kill ourselves.

Now study this example. A pregnant woman suffers from a rare form of cancer which responds well if chemotherapy begins immediately. Unfortunately, the therapy will likely kill her unborn fetus. Consider how starting the therapy satisfies the criteria.

1. The therapy, by itself, is not evil.

2. The evil effect--the death of the fetus--is *not* the means of achieving the good effect--saving her life. (Successful chemotherapy saves her life.)

3. She does not intend evil--the fetus' death. (She intends to save her life.)

4. She has a proportionate reason to save her life; it is incommensurably valuable.

On the other hand, compare this to abortion, which clearly violates the second criterion because the bad effect--the death of the fetus--achieves the good effect--saving them from caring for the child. It violates the third criterion because the pregnant woman intends the fetus' death and the fourth because whatever the reasons for the fetus' death, they do not sufficiently justify preventing its continued existence.

Take particular notice of how, in the last two cases, the resulting evil--the soldier's or the fetus' death--is unintended although it is a *foreseeable consequence*. Natural law theorists generally claim that a foreseeable consequence can be unintended. For example, if we receive an "F" on our ethics test the professor foresees our unhappiness, but this does not mean s/he intends our unhappiness. The professor may have simply graded our exam, or s/he may hope that the grade motivates us in the future. Most likely the professor believes that justice demands that students who work harder and study more merit better grades.

Take another example. We might foresee that telling our friend that she has glue on her nose will embarrass her. But we did not intend to embarrass her; we wanted her to wash her nose because she had an afternoon job interview. Or when we go jogging, we do not intend to wear out our running shoes, although we foresee this consequence. Thus, simply foreseeing a consequence does not mean it is intended.

Some argue that this is just semantics and detect no relevant distinction between intentions in the above cases. Thus our professor *does* intend to make us unhappy, and we *do* intend to embarrass our friend and wear out our running shoes. Some contemporary natural law ethicists defend the traditional view that, in the above cases, there are differences in intention. (Note that other contemporary natural law theorists have conceded that intention is not as critical as whether or not there is a proportionate reason for the bad effect. They ask, do we have a proportionately good reason to give just grades, embarrass our friend, and wear out our running shoes?)

Challenges to the double effect principle itself comes from those who argue that the ends *do* justify the means. Such theories focus primarily on consequences, whereas natural law theory concerns itself primarily with intentions. But intentions are problematic. How do we determine people's intentions? Do they really know our own intentions? Are human actions motivated by one intention or by a number of them? Can we distinguish between intrinsic and extrinsic intentions? How do we evaluate these cases of "mixed" intentions? These questions blur an otherwise lucid principle.

5. Ordinary and Extraordinary Means

The principle that life is both incommensurably valuable and a universal human good has important implications in areas like medical ethics. Specifically, it absolutely proscribes "mercy killing." In this century, Catholic theologians in the natural law tradition have introduced another relevant moral distinction particularly applicable in medical ethics: the distinction between ordinary and extraordinary means:

Ordinary means of preserving life are all medicines, treatments, and operations, which offer a reasonable hope of benefit for the patient and/or which can be obtained and used without excessive expense, pain, and other inconveniences.

Extraordinary means of preserving life are all those medicines, treatments, and operations which cannot be obtained without excessive expense, pain, or other inconvenience, or which, if used, would not offer a reasonable hope of benefit.

Although employment of extraordinary means is not morally obligatory, according to the principle, direct killing of an innocent human being or failing to provide ordinary measures to preserve life are *always wrong*. However, we can distinguish between ordinary medical means--treating pneumonia--and extraordinary moral means--treating pneumonia in a ninety-five year old patient with many other complications.

A number of difficulties arise concerning the distinction between ordinary and extraordinary means. In the first place, is it always wrong to withhold ordinary means? Do we continue to provide fluid for a patient who has been in a persistent vegetative state for a number of years? A second consideration refers to the demarcation between the two kinds of means. Just what is excessive? What is extraordinary? What is beneficial? Finally, no matter how one differentiates between the two, today's extraordinary treatment is likely to become tomorrow's ordinary one.

6. Some Philosophical Difficulties

Natural law theory derives values about what we ought to do from facts about our human nature. This is a major philosophical difficulty. When we derive what we *ought* to do from what *is* the case, we commit what philosophers call **the naturalistic fallacy**. This fallacy involves the derivation of ethical conclusions from non-ethical facts. Isn't there a logical gap between what is the case and what ought to be the case? Even if it *is* true, for instance, that humans are naturally aggressive, does that mean they *should* be? If you know that you are human; do you now know what to do in an ethical dilemma? Though a conception of human nature is not irrelevant to morality, it seems unlikely, many contemporary philosophers contend, that one could completely explain morality by appealing to human nature. Still, if values do not come from facts, "where do they come from?"

A second difficulty with the theory is that modern science rejects teleology. Explanations in science do not refer to goals, values, or purposes. Rocks do not fall because they desire the earth's center nor does it rain in order to make plants grow, as Aristotle supposed. Rather, physical reality operates according to impersonal laws of cause and effect, and thus, modern science rejects the natural law assumption that values and purposes are built into nature. Even our own bodies are the product of *random* genetic mutations and natural selection *after* the fact. Evolutionary theory, the fundamental theory of modern biology, rejects teleology and furthermore, according to contemporary cosmology, all of cosmic evolution results from a series of fortuitous occurrences. Nevertheless, a few contemporary biologists and cosmologists explain cosmic evolution with "theories of self-organization." Roughly speaking, these theories suggest that some type of self-organizational tendencies direct the evolutionary process, thereby questioning the concept of evolutionary randomness.

This brings to light a final difficulty. Contrary to biological evolution, natural law theory traditionally maintains the immutability of human nature, and, to be consistent with contemporary science, natural law must modify this claim. Perhaps an even greater challenge to the idea of the immutability of human nature comes from cultural evolution, whose technological manifestations--like medical equipment, artificial birth control, and genetic engineering--have implications for morality. Do the same moral principles apply before and after new technologies are developed?

Or do the options created by technology demand a rethinking of moral imperatives? Are individuals literally transformed when more choices become available to them?

No doubt, the most revolutionary example of the interaction between cultural evolution and human nature relates to areas of modern biology like gene-splicing and recombinant DNA. No longer will millions of years of biological evolution be needed to alter our nature; we may conceivably *alter our own nature*. When genetic engineering becomes that sophisticated, the idea of the immutability of human nature will be archaic. On the one hand, granted that human nature evolves, natural law theorists could simply modify their theory and argue that natural law applies relative to the state of human biological and cultural development. In fact, some contemporary natural law theorists base their ethics on an evolutionary model of human nature. On the other hand, such a theory would barely resemble its traditional form.

7. Final thoughts

Of course the fact that, with the exception of the Catholic Church, the theory of natural law has fallen into disfavor does not mean it is mistaken. If we presuppose or believe that we can philosophically demonstrate the existence of a source of values and purposes for human beings--and believe also that knowledge of this source is accessible to human reason--then one may rationally defend the theory. Furthermore, without such presuppositions, moral thinking is likely futile. A number of contemporary philosophers suggest that without some ultimate, objective source for morality, notions like obligation, duty, right, and good make no sense.

Nevertheless, natural law theory does rest upon a number of dubious philosophical propositions. We should not forget that, at least in the formulation of the Catholic Church, the natural law ultimately comes from God. Like the divine command theory, natural law ethics is open to all of the objections of philosophical theology. Is there a God? Are there any significant proofs for God's existence? Why is God so "hidden?" How do we know our reason is sufficient to understand God's natural moral laws? Moreover, a non-theistic natural law ethics must answer the challenge of the naturalistic fallacy. Why is the natural, good?

Whatever the conclusion, the gap between a non-teleological, factual, and scientific account of human nature and a teleological, ethical, and religious conception constitutes the central dispute in contemporary culture. We do not know how to reconcile the two poles, or if one or the other is bankrupt. But, as the historian of philosophy W.T. Jones asserts: "The whole history of philosophy since the seventeenth century is in fact hardly more than a series of variations on this central theme."

Chapter 4

The Social Contract

"The passions that incline [persons] to peace, are fear of death; desire of such things as are necessary to commodious living; and a hope by their industry to obtain them. And reason suggesteth convenient articles of peace, upon which [persons] may be drawn to agreement."
Thomas Hobbes

1. Hobbes and the Social Contract

Moving in western culture from the ancient and medieval periods into the sixteenth and seventeenth centuries, we approach modernity. The discovery of the new world, developments in commerce and industry, the Reformation, the scientific revolution, and the rise of the secular alongside the decline of Christianity transformed western civilization. Inevitably, natural law theory would be scrutinized. The major figures of the period-- Rene Descartes (1596-1650), Benedict de Spinoza (1632-1677), John Locke (1632-1704) and Gottfried Leibniz (1646-1716)--all tried, in one way or another, to reconcile the new secular ideas with traditional Christian morality. But the most revolutionary of all the new theorists was Thomas Hobbes (1588-1679), who believed that ethical norms were not to be found in God's cosmic plan but in our social and political agreements.

Hobbes detested violence. He had read Thucydides' account of the Peloponnesian War and had personally witnessed the decades of English civil war which culminated with the beheading of Charles II. The desire to avoid war motivated both his moral and political thought. Hobbes' philosophy began by considering what the world would be like without morality. He believed that it would be a **state of nature**; a terrible place without art, literature, commerce, industry, or culture. Most terrifying of all, it would be a place of "continual fear and danger of violent death; and the life of [humans] solitary, poor, nasty, brutish, and short." But why would it be so bad?

In the first place, Hobbes believed that human beings endeavor desperately to fulfill their *desires* for food, clothing, shelter, power, honor, glory, comfort, pleasure, self-aggrandizement, and a life of ease. Unfortunately, such things do not exist in abundance; they are *scarce*. In addition, he believed that persons were *relatively equal in their power*. Given desires, scarcity, relative power equality, and the predominant sense of *self-interest all human beings exhibit*, Hobbes concluded that human beings, in a state of nature, would be engaged in a fierce struggle over scarce resources. Individuals would attack, steal, destroy and invade to protect themselves and prove their status. Thus, Hobbes' *first thesis*: the state of nature is a state of war.

Hobbes' *second thesis* was that individuals in a state of nature have no *a priori* (natural, before experience) moral law that obligates them to constrain their behavior. For Hobbes, *self-preservation* justified the use of force and fraud to defend ourselves in a state of nature. In this state, only the power of others limited what we can do. Hobbes called this the *right of nature*. But this state is antithetical to our survival and so the desire for self-preservation expressed itself in another way which was Hobbes' *third thesis*: fear of death and the desire for a good life incline us toward peace. Hobbes called this the *law of nature*. Morality was defined by articles of peace, essentially, the rules to which any rational self-interested person would agree. The state of nature demands that we follow one of the two formulations of the self-preservation principle. In the state of nature, we should exercise our right of nature; in the state of peace, we should follow

the law of nature. These laws of nature bear no resemblance to the medieval concept of natural law; they simple demand self-preservation. In other words, *morality is the set of rules that make peaceful living possible.*

This led to Hobbes' *fourth thesis*: though it is in our own interest to *agree* to the articles of peace; it is not rational to *comply* with our agreements unless some coercive power forces us. Otherwise, we might feign agreement and, when the other complies, violate the accord. To prevent this, a coercive power must ensure that we comply with our agreements. This agreement between individuals to establish the laws that make communal living possible and an agency to enforce those laws is called **the social contract**.

2. A Theory of Morality

While issues surrounding the nature of the coercive agency which guarantees compliance with the social contract lead to political theory, the agreed-upon rules constitute morality. *Morality is the agreed-upon, mutually advantageous conventions which, assuming others' compliance, make society possible.* Thus, self-interest ultimately justifies morality. We can see easily that killing, lying, cheating, and stealing are prohibited since they threaten society and are not in anyone's self-interest. Whether the moral prohibitions against homosexuality, prostitution, abortion, or euthanasia are justified in terms of individual and societal interest is more debatable.

But whatever the agreed-upon rules, according to the theory they do not exist prior to human contracts. We *create* morality by our agreements within the constraints demanded by self-preservation and self-interest; we do not *discover* antecedent moral truths. Prior to the contract, actions are *neither* moral or immoral. But after the contract is signed, society forbids some actions, allows others, remains undecided on a few, and continually renegotiates the contract to satisfy rival parties. Therefore, the moral sphere is one of continual bargaining and power-struggling where conflict is resolved through moral discourse, a political mechanism or violence.

3. An "Actual" Contract

Following Hobbes, the contemporary Princeton philosopher Gilbert Harman has argued that morality consists of the moral conventions to which self-interested persons have **actually** agreed. To support his thesis, he shows how this view *explains* many otherwise inexplicable moral puzzles. For example, why do we take the duty not to harm others to be greater than the duty to help them? Harman proposes that this rule results from a real bargaining process between groups of unequal power. No group wants to be harmed, but the duty to help benefits the weakest groups. Since the weak are less powerful and influential in the bargaining process, the rich and powerful dictate that only a weak duty to help others will exist. In that way, the rich and powerful can be protected from harm by a strong duty but not inconvenienced by a strong duty to help others. Or consider that we have virtually no moral duties toward non-human animals. We can explain this easily if our moral relationships with animals arose through a bargaining process in which animals had no say. Thus, Harman contends that morality results from an actual contract between rational bargainers.

But what happens when we reach an impasse in the bargaining process or some moral puzzle appears unresolvable? Harman suggests that we begin by making explicit the role self-interest plays in moral bargaining. For example, the rich and powerful tend to emphasize freedom and property rights, while the poor and weak tend to emphasize equality. If self-interest was made more explicit, it would lend greater clarity and honesty to moral disputes.

Some more enigmatic moral disputes--say moral vegetarianism--revolve around principles other than self-interest. If moral rules are conventions, then all must accept that they have no privileged moral status when it comes to understanding morality. The vegetarians, as a group, share principles that most others do not. Since we do not violate the self-interest of vegetarians by eating meat, they should be tolerant of our practices.

Similarly, with abortion, if anti-abortionists admit they have no privileged access to moral truth, but accept principles that others do not, they will be inclined to be more tolerant. Of course, Harman admits abortion is a tougher case and that anti-abortion sentiment might survive a convention that dictates otherwise. But eventually we will reach a compromise, one favoring the pro-choice side, since self-interest plays a less significant role, Harman believes, for the pro-lifers. In other words, since morality is grounded ultimately in self-interest, moral rules that oppose people's interests will defer to more self-interested rules.

Harman's conclusion here exemplifies contractarian thinking; moral rules must be in an individual's self-interest and, if they are not, they will not ultimately survive because not enough individuals will be motivated to abide by them. In fact, the fundamental tenet of the contractarian approach to morality is that *any rule of social constraint is an arbitrary imposition upon us unless everyone's compliance can be shown to promote one individual's preferences, concerns, interests,* etc.

Of course there are those "unconditionally cooperative" individuals who will act altruistically whatever the cost and abide by their agreements even when it is not in their self-interest. They could be masochists! However, such individuals are in the minority. And there are other ways to justify non-self-interested actions to people. Religious, political, and familial institutions--as well as a number of philosophical arguments--have tried to convince persons to forego their self-interest for some greater good. Nevertheless, this has always been a difficult if not impossible task and, on the whole, not very successful. Consider how difficult it is--even with an enforcement agency in place--to prevent individuals from pursuing their self-interest. People cheat on their taxes even with enforcement in place! Perhaps morality would have a more firm foundation if one could demonstrate to all individuals that moral rules are in their self-interest. If moral rules cannot satisfy this requirement, then we have no reason to follow them. This emphasis on harnessing, rather than repressing, self-interested behavior is the hallmark of the contractarian approach.

4. Gauthier's Moral Philosophy

Another contemporary philosopher who follows in the tradition of Hobbes is David Gauthier of the University of Pittsburgh. In his influential text, *Morals By Agreement*, he argues that voluntary compliance with moral rules, even in the absence of enforcement, is in one's rational self-interest. Specifically, he contends that one should become a *constrained maximizer*, a person disposed to cooperate with others on the condition that they expect others to cooperate. We can all do better by voluntarily cooperating, considering the cost of establishing and maintaining enforcement agencies.

Like Harman, Gauthier contends that bargaining may resolve contract disputes, and he advances an entire bargaining theory to support this claim. Unlike Hobbes and Harman, Gauthier's moral theory depends less heavily on self-interest. If morality and self-interest coincide, Gauthier claims, then morality would be easy; we would just follow our interests. But this seems to be mistaken since morality and self-interest often conflict. Gauthier believes that morality calls upon us, at least sometime, to *constrain* ourselves from self-interested pursuits. On the other hand, he admits, if morality is not self-interested then you have no reason to be moral. It is from this paradox that morality derives.

What Gauthier has in mind echoes Hobbes. We must constrain ourselves to be moral, but because constraint allows us to live peacefully, it is ultimately self-interested. In the end, Gauthier agrees with both Harman and Hobbes that morality is grounded in self-interest and that moral constraint is the price we pay for a civilized society. But how exactly does Gauthier say that self-interest leads to morality?

5. Gauthier's Theory of Rationality

Gauthier develops his theory of morality as part of a theory of rational choice; in essence, morality is both self-interested and rational. We might begin by considering the conception of rationality central to his theory. For Gauthier, practical reason is strictly instrumental. This is sometimes called **the maximizing notion of rationality**. Accordingly, to be rational is to be disposed to act in a way that maximizes the satisfaction of one's interests, interests here are understood as one's considered, but nonetheless, subjectively determined preferences. On this conception of rationality, one's preferential interests need not be exclusively *in* the self, but preferential interests *of* the self, which may include interest in others.

The notion of rationality used here derives from that employed by economists in the classical tradition. The individual is the ultimate unit of analysis in this tradition. Individuals are assumed to make choices on the basis of their preferences and beliefs about the world. The choice is rational in this sense when it is consistent with those beliefs and preferences. Effects of human action and interaction are then explained as the intended or unintended outcomes of the individual choices producing it. As we will see, the effect of choices that are economical and, hence, individually rational may be nonetheless collectively harmful but at the same time avoidable.

Gauthier's prime rationale for employing a maximizing notion in attempting to provide morality with a rational foundation is to avoid begging questions, i.e., assuming what he's trying to prove. A maximizing notion has the advantage of being "weak" in the sense that it is least assuming about human nature or motivational structures; it makes no prior moral assumptions as do "strong" conceptions of rationality. Strong conceptions of rationality build morality into the conception of rationality. The weak conception of rationality has the advantage of generating moral constraint from a non-moral base.

Of course, to speak of maximizing anything presupposes that the item to be maximized is a measurable quantity. In respect of maximization, the measure of preference is called *utility*. Just as temperature is the measure of heat, utility is the measure of the preference of the individual. Note that since Gauthier assumes no value of possible states of affair other than that which is expressed in the utility measurement of individual preferences, his notion of value is both subjective and relative. The value of anything is a function of the individual's preference in respect of it. Rational choice entails maximizing utility or, more generally, acting in one's self-interest. In the moral sphere, we interact with other individuals and must take into consideration the actions of other parties. How does one make a rational (maximizing) choice in interactive situations?

6. Game Theory

To answer this question, we introduce the **theory of games**. For our purposes, a game is an interactive situation in which individuals, called players, choose strategies to deal with each other in attempting to maximize their individual utility. There are several ways of distinguishing games including: 1) in respect to the number of players involved; 2) in respect to the number of repetitions of play; 3) in respect of the order of the various player's preferences over the same outcomes. On the one extreme are games of pure conflict, so called zero-sum games, in which players have completely opposing interests over possible outcomes. On the other extreme are games of pure harmony, so-called games of coordination. In the middle are games involving both conflict and harmony in respect of others. It is one particular game that interests us most, since it describes the situation in Hobbes' state of nature, and is the central problem in contractarian moral theory.

7. The Prisoner's Dilemma

The **prisoner's dilemma** is one of the most controversial and widely debated situations in game theory. The story has implications for a variety of human interactive situations. A prisoner's dilemma is an interactive situation *in which it is better for all to cooperate rather than for no one to do so, yet it is best for each not to cooperate, regardless of what the others do.*

In the classic story, two prisoners have committed a serious crime but all of the evidence necessary to convict them is not admissible in court. Both prisoners are held separately and are unable to communicate. The prisoners are called separately by the authorities and each offered the same proposition. Confess and if your partner does not, you will be convicted of a lesser crime and serve one year in jail while the unrepentant prisoner will be convicted of a more serious crime and serve ten years. If you do not confess and your partner does, then it is you who will be convicted of the more serious crime and your partner of the lesser crime. Should neither of you confess the penalty will be two years for each of you, but should both of you confess the penalty will be five years. In the following matrix, you are the row chooser and your partner the column chooser. The first number in each parenthesis represents the "payoff" for you in years in prison, the second number your partner's years. Let us assume each player prefers the least number of years in prison possible. In matrix form, the situation looks like this:

		Prisoner 2	
		Confess	*Don't Confess*
Prisoner 1	*Confess*	(5, 5)	(1, 10)
	Don't Confess	(10, 1)	(2, 2)

So you reason as follows: If your partner confesses, you had better confess because if you don't you will get 10 years rather than 5. If your partner doesn't confess, again you should confess because you will only get 1 year rather than 2 for not confessing. So no matter what your partner does, you ought to confess. The reasoning is the same for your partner. The problem is that when both confess the outcome is worse for both than if neither confessed. You both could have done better, and neither of you worse, if you had not confessed! You might have made an agreement not to confess but this would not solve the problem. The reason is this: although agreeing not to confess is rational, compliance is surely not rational!

We have now come full circle to Hobbes. The prisoner's dilemma represents the situation in the state of nature. If the prisoners cooperate, they both do better; if they do not cooperate, they both do worse. But both have a good reason not to cooperate; they are not sure the other will! We can only escape this dilemma, Hobbes maintained, by installing a coercive power that makes us comply with our agreements (contracts). Gauthier argues, as we saw earlier, for the rationality of voluntary uncoerced cooperation and compliance with agreements given the costs to each of us of enforcement agencies. We need to embrace what he calls "morals by agreement."

8. Contemporary Application

In the last chapter, we discussed how natural law theory applied to issues in medical ethics. Let us do the same with contract theory. We see easily the large role contracts play in our society, in our marriages, in transference of our property, etc. For example, *the advanced directives for health care* specify the contract rights of individuals to exercise personal autonomy *vis-a-vis* doctors and hospitals. These directives give individuals a legal right, backed up by the coercive power of the state, to sign "living wills" which direct the kinds of treatment they desire.

They also provide for individuals to assign "durable power of attorney" to apply when they can no longer speak for themselves. This circumvents the problem of weak rationality and demonstrates how contracts function in the real world, since these codes were the result of bargaining between various groups. Similarly, contractarians would probably allow euthanasia, or other morally questionable activities, to be performed between voluntary rational cooperators. This theory brings us closest to the convergence of the legal and moral because we often resolve delicate moral issues with voluntary contracts between rational parties. Moral bargaining decides which contracts are allowable.

9. Objections

But does morality merely consist in the set of rules that rational, self-interested people agree to because they are mutually beneficial? Is that all there is to morality? There are a number of intricate complications surrounding a social contract theory of morality, but two fundamental, yet intertwined, objections continually recur: first, that humans are not relative power equals; and second, that the theory conflicts with ordinary moral consciousness because it does not allow for "weak rationals." We will consider each objection in turn.

If humans are not relatively equal in their power, as Hobbes and his predecessors suppose, then the theory degenerates into "might makes right." When contract theorists say that humans are relative power equals, they mean that no one person or persons can dominate another person or group for very long because the dominated parties will rise up, unite, and overthrow their oppressors.

At first glance, history would seem to both confirm and deny this assumption. On the one hand, dominated parties continually rise up and, through violence or contract renegotiation, revise social contracts. On the other hand, groups have been dominated for very long times. The long history of domination, oppression, and enslavement suggest that persons are not always relative power equals. Thus, the assumption that they are is tenuous at best and, if it is not true, the chances for a contract theory representing anything like our common sense morality is slim. Some theorists, like Harman for instance, admit that the contract is tilted in favor of the powerful. Nevertheless, if humans are radically unequal in their power, then the moral contract between unequal parties will never approximate common sense morality because strong parties will always have their way.

The other related difficulty has to do with so-called "weak rationals," including non-human animals, the mentally retarded, children, and others who are incapable of participating in or understanding a social contract. Inasmuch as our ordinary moral intuitions suggest that we have obligations toward weak rationals, either the theory or our moral intuitions are mistaken. Weak rationals exemplify the idea of power inequality. (Others, like technological inferiors, may be unequal in their power because of cultural, not personal defect; we might call such persons "weak culturals.") Unless we can devise some way to reconcile contractarianism with our ordinary moral intuitions--that weak rationals and relative power unequals deserve moral consideration--then, assuming our intuitions are reliable, contract theory is seriously flawed. There are a number of possible replies by the contractarian.

10. Possible Replies

First, they might argue that power unequals are *not* worthy of moral consideration. This argument might be given plausibility by considering how the society loses precious resources in caring for and accommodating itself to weak rationals. The argument would be enormously complex and politically volatile, and its prescriptions reminiscent of Social Darwinism. Needless to say, most would dismiss this argument out of hand. Of course, as with natural law theory, the fact that few defend a particular view does not mean it is mistaken.

Second, contractarians could modify their theory as follows. Since we need to constrain our interests for the common good, and since self-interest pulls us in the opposite direction, it is a good idea for all of us to habitualize the kinds of behavior that make the social contract possible. If we treat weak rationals any way we like, we might habitualize socially destructive behaviors, instead of the kinds of actions that make social living possible. For instance, there seems to be no legitimate reason not to kick our dog, according to the social contract, if doing so makes us feel better. But the modified version of the contract supplies an excellent reason why we shouldn't do this; we might begin to release our aggression against contractors as well and hasten the descent back into the state of nature. How well we could adumbrate this modified theory is unknown. If we could do it well enough, we might repair the theory's apparent defect. But if not, contract theory will almost certainly be rejected as both an explanation and a justification for morality.

11. John Rawls

We might also suggest the approach of the Harvard philosopher John Rawls, whose book *A Theory of Justice* is the single most influential philosophical ethics text of the past quarter century. Rawls' contractarian approach differs radically from the approach of either Gauthier or Harman because it finds its inspiration, not in Hobbes, but in Locke, Rousseau, and Kant. (We examine Locke and Kant in later chapters.)

Rawls begins by considering the *original position* where parties deliberate about the rules of right conduct that will be universally applicable in society. In the bargaining position, parties are impartial, that is, everyone's interest count equally. This is guaranteed by the so-called *veil of ignorance* that hides from contractors any knowledge of themselves. You do not know your race, sex, social class, or nationality from behind the veil of ignorance. Although parties are self-interested and want to establish rules beneficial for themselves, in reality, self-interest is ruled out by the veil of ignorance because from behind it one cannot differentiate their interests from the interest's of others.

The rules agreed to by rational bargainers behind a veil of ignorance are moral rules. This solution demonstrates a hypothetical way that contract theory could account for the rules favored by ordinary moral consciousness, since the veil of ignorance assures us that impartial rules will result. However, by mitigating the role played by self-interest, this type of contract radically departs from the account of morality given by Hobbes or any neo-Hobbesians.

12. Conclusion

In conclusion, it appears that contract theory is viable to the extent that individuals are relatively equal in power when the contract is both negotiated and renegotiated. But, in the real world, this does not appear to be the case. Thus, we always have an imperfect contract which represents the interests of the stronger, more interested, or more persuasive parties. Whether an "equilibrium" can be reached in the bargaining process is problematic. Individuals rarely encounter each other "on a level playing field" even when interacting within the contract. So even though it may be the case that morality is, as Harman supposes, nothing more than the result of bargaining and power-struggling between various groups, we can still ask whether this *should be the case.* Many accept the "is" but reject the "ought." And if they do, then morality "ought to be" more than just a contract between rational bargainers.

In conclusion, let us note how much of contemporary western civilization operates within a contract framework. We have contracts that govern our property, our mortgages, and our marriages. We have contracts that state who will speak for us if we cannot speak for ourselves and what kind of medical technology is deemed appropriate to sustain our lives. In short, we are a contract society. Whether this is for the better, only the reader can judge.

Chapter 5

Deontological Ethics

"Now suppose [they] tear [themselves], unsolicited by inclination, out of this dead insensibility and to perform this action only from duty and without any inclination--then for the first time [their] action has genuine moral worth."
Immanuel Kant

1. Kant and Hume

The German philosopher Immanuel Kant (1724-1804), called by many the greatest of modern philosophers, was the preeminent defender of **deontological** (duty) ethics. He lived such an austere and regimented life that the people of his town were reported to have set their clocks by the punctuality of his walks. He rose at 4 a.m., studied, taught, read, and wrote the rest of the day. He was an accomplished astronomer, mathematician, metaphysician, one of the most celebrated epistemologists and ethicians of all time, and, in many ways, the crowning figure of the Enlightenment. During the Enlightenment, European civilization celebrated the idea that human reason was sufficient to understand, interpret, and restructure the world. Perhaps the greatest rationalist ever, Kant defended this view in both his epistemology and ethics.

To understand Kant, we might briefly consider his immediate predecessor David Hume (1711-1776). Hume had awakened Kant "from his dogmatic slumber," forcing him to reconsider all of his former beliefs. Hume's skepticism had challenged everything for which the Enlightenment stood, and he was, perhaps, the greatest and most consistent skeptic the Western world had yet produced. He argued that Christianity was nonsense, that science was uncertain, that the source of sense experience was unknown, and that ethics was purely subjective.

Specifically, Hume believed that moral judgments express our sentiments or feelings and that morality was based upon an innate sympathy we have for our fellow human beings. If humans possess the proper sentiments, they were moral; if they lack such sympathies, they were immoral. Thus, Hume continued the attack on authority and tradition--an attack characteristic of the Enlightenment--but *without* the Enlightenment's faith in reason. In particular, he criticized the view that morality was based upon reason which, according to Hume, can tell us about facts, but never tell us about values. In short, reason is practical; it determines the means to some end. But ends come from desires and sentiments, not from reason. In vivid contrast to natural law theory, our ends, goals, and purposes depend upon our passions and, consequently, no passions are irrational. Hume made these points in a few famous passages: "Reason is, and ought only to be the slave of the passions...[Thus]...Tis not contrary to reason to prefer the destruction of the whole world to the scratching of my finger."

Hume's skepticism stunned Kant. What of the Enlightenment's faith in reason? If desire preceded reason, and desires cannot be irrational, then Enlightenment rationalism was dead. How can we reestablish faith in reason? How can we show that some passions and inclinations are irrational? In his monumental work *The Critique of Pure Reason*, Kant attempted to elucidate the rational foundations of both the natural and mathematical sciences, defending reason against Hume's onslaught. He then turned his attention to establishing a foundation for ethics in *The Critique of Practical Reason*. If morality were subjective, as Hume thought, then the concept of an objective moral law was a myth. And if no passions were irrational, then anything goes in morality. In essence, Kant needed to answer Hume's subjectivism and irrationalism by demonstrating the rational foundations of the moral law.

2. Freedom and Rationality

Kantian philosophy is enormously complex and obscure. Yet, Kant's basic ideas are surprisingly simple. His most basic presupposition was his belief in human freedom. While the natural world operates according to laws of cause and effect, he argued, the moral world operates according to self-imposed "laws of freedom." We may reconstruct one of his arguments for freedom as follows:

1. Without freedom, morality is not possible.
2. Morality exists, thus
3. Freedom exists.

The first premise follows if we consider how determinism undermines morality. (See chapter 2) The second premise Kant took as self-evident, and the conclusion follows logically from the premises. But where does human freedom come from? Kant believed that freedom came from rationality, and he advanced roughly the following argument to support this claim:

1. Without reason, we would be slaves to our passions
2. If we were slaves to our passions, we would not be free; thus
3. Without reason, we would not be free.

Together, we now have the basis upon which to cement the connection between reason and morality.

1. Without reason, there is no freedom
2. Without freedom, there is no morality, thus
3. Without reason, there is no morality.

Kant believed moral obligation derived from our free, rational nature. But how should we exercise our freedom? What should we choose to do?

3. Intention, Duty, and Consequences

Kant began his most famous work in moral philosophy with these immortal lines: "Nothing in the world--indeed nothing even beyond the world --can possibly be conceived which could be called good without qualification except a good will." For Kant, a good will freely conformed itself and its desires to the moral law. That is its **duty!** Nevertheless, the moral law does not force itself upon us, we must freely choose to obey it. For Kant, *the intention to conform our free will to the moral law, and thereby do our duty, is the essence of morality.*

The emphasis on the agent's **intention** brings to light another salient issue in Kant's ethics. *So long as the intention of an action is to abide by the moral law, then the consequences are irrelevant.* For instance, if you try valiantly to save someone from a burning building but are unsuccessful, no one holds you responsible for your failure. Why? Because your intention was good. The reverse is also true. If I intend to harm you, but inadvertently help you, I am still morally culpable. Kant gave his own example to dramatize the role intention played in morality. Imagine shopkeepers who would cheat their customers given the opportunity, but who do not *only* because it is bad for business. In other words, the shopkeepers do the right thing only because the **consequences** are good. If they could cheat their customers without any repercussions, they would do so. According to Kant, these shopkeepers are not moral. On the other hand, shopkeepers who gave the correct change out of a sense of duty are moral.

The emphasis on the agent's intention captures another important idea in deontology, the emphasis on the right over good. Right actions are done in accordance with duty; they do not promote values like happiness or the common good. Kant makes it clear that dutiful conduct does not necessarily make us happy. In fact, it often makes us unhappy! We should do the right thing because it is our duty, not because it makes us happy. *If we want to be happy, he says, we should follow our instincts*, since instinct is a better guide to happiness than reason.

But morality cannot rest upon passions. If it did, morality would be both subjective and relative. For ethics to be objective, absolute, and precise--to be like the sciences--it needs to be based upon reason. Only the appeal to the objectivity of reason allows us to escape the subjectivity of the passions. In summary, *a good will intends to do its duty and follows the moral law without consideration of the consequences.*

4. Hypothetical Imperatives

But what exactly does reason command? We have already seen how reason commands actions *given antecedent desires*. If we want a new car, then reason tells us the various means to achieve this end. We can save or borrow the money, pray, enter a raffle, call our mother, or steal a car. But whatever we do, reason only tells us how to pursue the end; it does not tell us which ends are worth pursuing. Commands or imperatives of this sort, Kant called **hypothetical imperatives**, since they depend upon some desires or interests that we happen, hypothetically, to have.

Kant distinguished between two types of hypothetical imperatives. The type we have been discussing so far, what he called "rules of skill," demand a definite means to a contingent (dependent) end. There are also what Kant called "counsels of prudence," which are contingent means to a definite end. Kant recognized that happiness was a common end or universal goal for all individuals, but that the means to this end was uncertain. For example, we may think that getting a new car or losing weight will make us happy, but when we get the new car or figure we may still be unhappy. Even though the end is definite, the means to the end are not. Thus, there are no universal hypothetical imperatives because either the ends are contingent or the means to the end are uncertain.

5. The Categorical Imperative

Does reason command anything absolutely? In other words, does reason issue any imperatives which do not depend upon contingent ends or uncertain means? Hume had claimed that reason did not command in this way and that any rational commands depend upon our passions. But if absolute commands exist--commands independent of personal taste--then the essence of the moral law is revealed.

If we think about any law--say temporal relativity--we recognize immediately that law is characterized by its universal applicability. So that, if relativity theory is true, then time is relative to motion everywhere throughout the universe. Similarly, the distributive law of mathematics applies no matter what numbers we insert into it or what planet we are on. Mundane physical laws are similar. Suppose we are asked about the post-operative effects of aspirin. We do not know about the anti-clotting effects of aspirin and believe it should be given after operations. In this example, it seems clear that the truth of the matter does not depend upon us; it depends upon laws governing how human bodies respond to aspirin. Kant believed that the moral law was like this. If there really is a reason why killing innocent people is wrong, then the reason applies universally. It doesn't matter that we want, desire, or like to kill innocent persons; we violate the moral law by doing so.

Of course, we can *say* that killing innocent people does not violate the moral law just as we can say that time is not relative to motion, that the distributive law works only on Monday, or that aspirin should only be given after operations. But our statements do not effect these laws; rather, the laws determine the truth of our statements. Kant held that a universally applicable moral law governs human behavior and can be discovered by human reason.

Kant had seized upon the idea of universalization as the key to the moral law. He called the first and most famous formulation of the moral law **the categorical imperative:** *"Act only according to that maxim by which you can at the same time will that it should become a universal law."* A maxim is a subjective principle of action which reveals our intention. To universalize a maxim is simply to ask, "what if everybody did this?" We should act according to a principle which we can universalize with consistency or without inconsistency. By testing the principle of our actions in this way, we determine if they are moral. If we can universalize our actions without any inconsistency, then they are moral; if we cannot do so, they are immoral. Ponder these simple examples. There is no logical inconsistency in universalizing the maxim, whenever we need a car we will work hard to earn the money. However, there is something inconsistent about universalizing the maxim, whenever we need a car we will steal it.

Kant advanced five formulations of the same imperative. Another famous formulation was: *"Act so that you treat humanity, whether in your own person or in that of another, always as an end and never merely as a means."* This formulation introduces us to the idea of respect for persons. Individuals are not a means to an end; we should not use people. Instead, they are ends in themselves with their own goals and purposes. Whether we use ourself or others, we violate the imperative if we treat any human being without dignity and respect. Certainly it is true that we all use people to an extent. We use physicians, teachers, nurses, and auto mechanics to get what we want. But there is a difference between paying persons for services and using them merely as a means to your end. In the latter case, we disregard their inherent worth.

6. Perfect and Imperfect Duties

The categorical imperative commands actions in two different ways. It specifically forbids or requires certain actions, and it commands that certain general goals be pursued. The former are called *perfect duties,* the latter *imperfect duties*. Perfect duties include: do not lie, do not kill inno- cent persons, and do not use people. We should never perform these actions! Imperfect duties include: helping others, developing our talents, and treating others with respect. These duties are absolute, but the way we satisfy them varies. There is flexibility in how we help others, treat them with respect, or develop our talents. When we universalize a maxim that violates a perfect duty, we will an inconsistent world. When we univer- salize a maxim that violates an imperfect duty, we will an unpleasant world.

7. Kant's Examples

Kant provided four examples--making false promises, committing sui- cide, developing our talents, and helping others--to demonstrate how the categorical imperative governs human conduct. Consider Kant's *first* ex- ample, making a false promise. Can we consistently will the principle, "whenever in need of money make a false promise to get it?" We cannot, since a world where everyone acts according to this maxim would be inconsistent. This is easy to demonstrate. In such a world: 1) false promises would be useful because there would be persons to believe them; and 2) false promises would not be useful because, in a short time, nobody would believe them. Such a world is *not even possible*. On the one hand, it would contain the necessary preconditions for false promises to be successful--people to believe our lies--and, on the other hand, the normal and predictable result of universal false promising would be that no lies would be believed. So it is not just that this world is unpleasant; it is logically impossible!

Consider Kant's *second* example. Imagine that we are depressed and contemplate suicide. Our principle of action is "whenever we are depressed we will commit suicide." Now try to universalize a world in which everyone does this. What would it be like? In such a world: 1) people would exist to commit suicide; and 2) people would not exist to commit the suicides they intend. Such a world is not logically possible. On the one hand, it would contain the necessary preconditions of suicide--live people to commit the act--and, on the other hand, the normal and predictable result of universal suicide would be that everyone would be dead. It is easy to think of other examples. Worlds where everyone were killers or bank robbers would be logically impossible in the same way. Kant had demonstrated, at least to his own satisfaction, that these actions were both immoral and irrational!

If we consider the same two actions--making false promises and suicide--in terms of the second formulation of the categorical imperative, we discover that they violate it as well. If we make a false promise to someone, then we use that person as a means to our end. Analogously, if we commit suicide, then we use ourself to achieve some end. When universalization of a maxim is inconsistent or when we use ourself or others, we violate perfect duties. Kant believed that telling the truth and not committing suicide exemplify perfect duties. There are no exceptions to them.

Kant believed we have a moral obligation to develop our talents, which was his *third* example. Suppose we are comfortable and prefer to indulge ourselves rather than develop our talents. We act according to this maxim: "since we are reasonably well-off, we won't develop our talents." Upon reflection, we recognize that failure to develop our talents violates a duty and could not be universalized consistently. For if everyone failed to develop their natural talents, they would not fulfill the purpose for which those talents exist.

Furthermore, he might have added, nothing useful would be accomplished in human society without the development of talent. Yet, Kant never claimed such a world was impossible, unimaginable, or logically inconsistent. Rather, rational persons cannot will this maxim to be a universal law without disastrous and unpleasant results.

Similarly, we have a moral obligation to help others, Kant's *fourth* example. Suppose we are prosperous and care little for others. We violate a duty by not helping others, and we cannot universalize the maxim. For we may need the benefit of others in the future. Again, Kant did not say this world was impossible, but he did not think any rational person desired such a world.

If we consider the same two actions--developing our talents and helping others--in terms of the second formulation of the categorical imperative, we discover similar difficulties. When universalization of a maxim has disastrous results or when we fail to treat ourselves and others as ends, we violate imperfect duties. Therefore, developing our talents and helping others are imperfect duties. They are absolute duties, but the specific means by which we satisfy these duties are open.

We may say that *the categorical imperative is the formal representation of the moral law to the human mind.* It commands human conduct independent of context. Compare the categorical imperative, as an abstract formulation of the moral law, to the distributive law in mathematics. This law states: $a(b+c)=ab+ac$. As stated, the principle is merely formal and without content. We give it content by putting numbers into the equation. The categorical imperative functions similarly in the moral domain. There, we place the maxim that operates in the moral context (situation) into the formulation to determine what to do. When we want to steal a library book or trash the sidewalk we ask, "what if everybody did this?" Recognizing the negative implications of our maxim, we see how it violates the categorical imperative. Theoretically, we may place any principle into the formulation to determine its morality. Those who do not test their maxim in this manner, turn away from the moral law.

8. Contemporary Applications

Let us consider a contemporary application of deontology to medical ethics. The emphasis on truth telling precludes lying by health care professionals to their patients or research subjects. Imperfect duties such as beneficence are straightforward, but how we help others is vague. The permissibility of euthanasia is also problematic. On the one hand, we may be able to universalize some forms of euthanasia or physician-assisted suicide, but, on the other hand, suicide is unequivocally forbidden. Thus, the permissibility of euthanasia depends in large part on how suicide is interpreted. The respect for persons notion is equally vague, since it is not clear what it entails. Again, we are prohibited from treating ourselves or others as means, yet we should respect our's and others' autonomy.

9. Problems with Universalization

Despite its initial plausibility, universalization is problematic. For one thing, it is easy to universalize immoral maxims. Suppose we act according to the maxim, "Catholics should be exterminated." There is no problem universalizing this maxim, in fact, we hope it does become universal if we really hate Catholics. The maxim "always kill Catholics," just like the maxim "never kill Catholics," can be universalized without contradiction by consistent Catholic-haters. Therefore, the test for universalization cannot discriminate between the two actions. We can also universalize a non-moral action like, "whenever we are alone, we sing." We may universalize this without contradiction, but that does not mean it is moral.

It is also easy enough to think of non-moral and supposedly moral maxims which *cannot* be universalized. We cannot universalize maxims like, "whenever hungry, go to Sue's diner," or "whenever we want to go to school, go to *our* school." It is not possible for *everyone* to go Sue's diner or our school. More significantly, many moral actions cannot be universalized. We cannot universalize the maxim, "sell all you have and follow the Lord." If everyone is selling, no one is buying! We cannot even universalize a simple maxim like, "put other people first," since everyone cannot be last! (The so-called altruist's dilemma.) So the test for universalization does not seem to adequately distinguish moral from immoral actions.

This brings to light a related difficulty. What maxim must we test for universalization? Maxims vary according to their generality or specificity. Kant tested very general maxims for universalization. "We cannot lie to achieve an end." Suppose we made the maxim more specific. "We cannot lie except to save innocent people from murder." This maxim is universalizable and spares us from telling the truth to inquiring murderers who ask the whereabouts of their intended victims. We could make the maxim even more specific. "We cannot lie except to save innocent people from murder and to spare people's feelings." The problem is that as maxims become more specific, more questionable maxims become capable of consistent universalization. Eventually, we would be testing very specific maxims. Suppose a bald, bearded, philosopher professor, Horatio Rumplestilskin, was about to steal a book from the college library on Thursday at 12:22 p.m. He would discover, upon careful examination, that he could universalize a world where all so named and described individuals stole books at precisely that time. If maxims become this specific, universalization has no meaning. Thus, maxims must have some generality to be properly tested.

Now suppose I test the following maxim. "We cannot lie except to achieve our ends." This maxim is sufficiently general to be universalized, but not sufficiently specific to rule out immoral actions. And the problem is not ameliorated by turning to the second formulation of the imperative. Does respect for persons tell us anything about whether we should universalize general or specific maxims? Should I always respect persons or always respect them except in certain situations? It appears that universalization is not as simple as it initially appeared.

10. General Difficulties

Kant claimed that duties are *absolute*. If duties are absolute, then what about conflicts between duties? Kant states that perfect duties supersede imperfect ones, and thus the duty not to lie precedes the duty to help others. If this is so, it follows that we must tell the truth to inquiring murderers. But this presented great difficulties for Kant. Surely duties have exceptions and perfect duties are not sacrosanct. Kant might have avoided this difficulty, as we have seen, by advocating that we universalize maxims with exceptions. A maxim like, "never lie except to inquiring murderers," is not problematic.

Along these lines, the twentieth-century philosopher W.D. Ross argued that no duties were absolute. Ross, who taught at Oxford for nearly fifty years and was one of the world's great Aristotelian and Kantian scholars, tried to modify Kant's theory to account for conflict of duty cases. According to Ross, we have *prima facie*--at first glance--duties, but they are conditional. Our actual duties--at second glance, you might say--depend upon the situation. In conflict of duty cases, we carefully weigh our duties and then proceed to do the best we can. The problem is whether Ross' conception of duties is too subjective and situational, since individuals decide which duties apply in given situations. The main problem with Ross' version of deontology is its emphasis on subjects and situations, an emphasis Kant wanted to avoid.

Another problem with Kant's system is that it is so formal and abstract it hardly motivates us. Even if Kant could prove that ethics were completely rational, wouldn't this take something away from the importance of moral choice? Isn't ethics too messy and imprecise for the formality, precision, and logic of Kant's system? Aristotle said that ethics could never be so precise. Maybe Kant demanded too much precision from his ethics?

Another general difficulty is deontology's rejection of the importance of consequences. According to Kant, if we do our duty we are absolved of all responsibility for the consequences of our action. He defends this view in part because he believes we can never know the consequences with certainty. This is true to an extent, but this view rests upon very pessimistic assumptions about our knowledge of the consequences of our actions. If for no apparent reason we tell our friend she looks positively awful and disgusting, we can be pretty sure she will feel bad about this. We are hardly absolved by our claim that we were not sure she would feel bad. Sometimes we can be reasonably sure of the consequences, in which case duty may not be important. Much trouble has been caused by people who were simply "doing their duty."

11. Kant's Fundamental Idea

Despite the nuances connected with the idea of universalization, there is a core idea at the heart of Kant's theory which is his lasting legacy. We have all been reprimanded by someone saying "how would you like someone to do that to you?" This is Kant's fundamental idea. If there is a reason why you don't want people to do something to you, then that same reason applies to what you want to do to others. It gives you a reason not to treat others in a way that you do not want to be treated. And, if you ignore that reason, you are acting irrationally. This is the kind of rational constraint Kant believed imposed itself upon our conduct. Of course, we have all experienced people who believe that the rules that apply to us do not apply to them, and, if they are bigger or more powerful than we are there is not much we can do. They might say to us, "You help me move on Saturday, but I won't help you move next week." We feel that they are doing something unfair and inconsistent, whether or not they recognize it. That is Kant's fundamental idea. A reason for one is a reason for all.

A purely rational morality is a fascinating idea. We saw in an earlier chapter how moral judgments might be truths of reason. Whether this is true depends upon our understanding of concepts like rationality, interests, and individuality. In the strong conception of rationality, others' interests give us a reason to act. In the weak conception, others' interests do not give us a reason. This issue also relates to the earlier discussion of egoism between Kalin and Medlin. If we think other people should respect our interests, so the argument goes, then we should respect theirs. But when we say others should respect our interests does that mean: 1) we want them to respect our interests; or 2) they have a reason to respect our interests. Kant, and his contemporary followers argue for "2," while other philosophers argue for "1." Clearly we want others to act in our interest, but it is not clear our interests give others a reason to act.

A conception of individualism is also relevant. If we have a strong conception of individuality--one in which individuals are radically separate--it is hard to see how the other's desires/interests/wants give us a reason to do anything. On the other hand, if we have a weak conception of individuality --one in which all individuals are intimately connected--it is easy to see how the other's interests give us reason to act. Maybe the rise of individualism lessens our sense of obligation toward others, or maybe communalism lessens our sense of obligation toward ourselves. Whatever our conclusions, the conceptions of rationality, interests, and individuality play a significant role in determining whether Kant's primary idea is convincing for us.

Kant's basic idea is that morality is grounded in reason. Essentially, if there really is a reason why we should not commit immoral acts, then that reason applies to all of us. If there really is a reason to treat people with dignity and respect, or not to lie or cheat them, then this reason applies to all of us whether we want it to or not. To say there are universal moral reasons ultimately confirms our belief in the intelligibility of reality. And, if the moral universe is unintelligible, nothing matters.

12. Conclusion

Despite all the positive contributions of Kant's moral thought, one final difficulty plagues the theory. Kant argued that the good life is a life of duty and that other lives are not worthwhile. But there have been many decent and happy lives that were not motivated by duty. Consider also persons who live from a sense of duty, but who are miserable and unhappy. They live without love, compassion, pleasure, beauty, or intellectual stimulation. Are such individuals moral exemplars? True, many live decadent lives in exclusive pursuit of pleasure or happiness while dismissing moral virtue. But Kant's ethics suffer from its emphasis on duty and virtue while neglecting happiness and pleasure. And if a philosophy stresses duty over happiness, then why should we do our duty? Duty may be part of morality, but so is happiness . We now turn to a moral theory which emphasizes the good over the right, happiness over duty.

Chapter 6

Utilitarianism

"...the Greatest Happiness Principle, holds that actions are right in proportion as they tend to promote happiness, wrong as they tend to produce the reverse of happiness."
John Stuart Mill

1. Utility and Happiness

Jeremy Bentham (1748-1832), who lived in London during the Industrial Revolution, was a philosopher and social reformer who wished to alleviate the period's dreadful living conditions. Poverty, disease, overcrowding, child labor, lack of sanitation, and miserable prison and factory conditions inspired Bentham to be an agent of social reform. He graduated from Oxford at the age of fifteen and used his prodigious gifts as social critic and legal and constitutional reformer. He became the leader of a group of individuals, including James Mill (1773-1836) and John Stuart Mill (1806-1873), who espoused the principles of a moral philosophy called **utilitarianism**. Utilitarianism was an influential force in eighteenth- and nineteenth-century England, and Bentham personally influenced the British legislature to adopt virtually all of his proposals.

The guiding principle of Bentham's thought was the **principle of utility**: *human actions and social institutions should be judged right or wrong depending upon their tendency to promote the pleasure or happiness of the greatest number of people.* A popular formulation of the principle is "promote the greatest happiness for the greatest number." Bentham himself defined the principle of utility as "that principle which approves or disapproves of every action whatsoever, according to the tendency which it appears to have to augment or diminish the happiness of the party whose interest is in question." Bentham was not clear as to whether the principle referred to the utility of individual actions or classes of actions, but he was clear "the party whose interest is in question" refers to "anything that can suffer." Thus, utilitarianism was the first moral philosophy to give a significant place to non-human animals.

Utility measures the happiness or unhappiness that results from a particular action. The **net utility** measures the balance of the happiness over the unhappiness or, in other words, the balance of an action's good and bad results. To compute the net utility, we subtract the unhappiness caused by an action from the happiness it causes. If an action produces more happiness than unhappiness, a *positive net utility* results. If it produces more unhappiness than happiness, a *negative net utility* results.

When deciding upon a course of action utilitarians take the following steps. First, they determine the available courses of action. Second, they add up all the happiness and unhappiness caused by each action. Third, they subtract the unhappiness from the happiness of each action resulting in the net utility. Finally, they perform that action from the available alternatives which has most net utility. (Technically, this is "act" utilitarianism, to be distinguish from another type shortly.)

If all of the available actions produce a positive net utility, or if some produce positive and some produce negative net utility, utilitarians perform the action that produces the most positive utility. If all the available actions produce a negative net utility, then they perform the one with the least negative utility. In summary, utilitarians perform that action which produces the greatest balance of happiness over unhappiness from the available alternatives. Thus, *the first key concept of utilitarianism is that of maximizing utility or happiness*.

It is important to note that computations of the net utility count *everyone's happiness equally.* Unlike egoists, who claim that persons should maximize their own utility, utilitarians do not place their own happiness above that of others. For example, egoism recommends that we insult others if that makes us happy, but utilitarianism does not. For utilitarians, the happiness we experience by insulting them is more than balanced by the injury they endure. Analogously, robbing banks, killing people, and not paying our taxes may make us happy, but these actions decrease the net utility. Therefore, utilitarianism does not recommend any of them.

Utilitarianism is a doctrine which grips the imagination of most twentieth-century people. Nearly all newspaper columnists, politicians, social reformers, and ordinary citizens believe that we should "make the world a better place," "increase social justice," "promote the general welfare," "establish equality," or "create the greatest happiness for the most people." Utilitarian thinking underlies most of these phrases, and many individuals believe they are morally obligated to increase the happiness and decrease the unhappiness in the world.

2. The Consequences

The second key concept of utilitarianism is that we judge moral actions by the consequences they produce. The only thing that counts in morality is the happiness and unhappiness produced by an action. In other words, according to utilitarianism, *the ends justify the means.* It does not matter how you do it--what means you take--as long as you increase the net utility. In most cases, as we have already mentioned, the action that utilitarians recommend mimics the recommendations of other moral theories. For instance, given the choice of telling Sue that she looks beautiful or terrible, we would usually maximize utility by telling her the former. Similarly, given the choice of granting or denying her request for a loan, we would usually maximize utility by granting her request. However, if she will probably use the money to buy drugs, become intoxicated and then beat her children, we should deny her request. On the other hand, if Bob will use our money to feed his children, we should probably loan it to him. We should always perform that action that will, most likely, increase the happiness and decrease the misery of all involved.

Since the right action depends upon our assessment of the consequences, we must know what the consequences of our actions will be. Some object that the theory fails precisely because this is not possible. And it is true that we never know *absolutely* what will happen as a consequence of our action. We may think the consequence of loaning Bob some money will be to cheer him up, but he might buy a gun and commit suicide! We may think the consequence of shooting Sue will be to hurt or kill her. But her subsequent paralysis might serve as the motivation for a successful writing career! In fact, any of our minuscule choices might alter human history, but we are only responsible for consequences we can reasonably anticipate. We anticipate the consequences as best we can and proceed to act accordingly. Thus, the fact that we can never be absolutely certain of the consequences of an act does not undermine utilitarianism.

We can now summarize our discussion thus far. Moral actions are those that produce the best consequences. The best consequences are those that have the most net utility, in other words, those that increase happiness and decrease unhappiness. When calculating the net utility everyone's interests count equally. The two key concepts of utilitarianism are happiness and consequences.

3. Examples of Utilitarian Reasoning

Consider this complex situation. Our teacher arrives the first day of class and makes the following announcement. "Let's not have class all semester! We will not inform the authorities and we will keep it a secret. None of us will do any work. I will not have to teach, and you do not have to study. I will give you each an 'A,' and you can give me excellent teaching evaluations. All of us will be happy and the net utility increased. Any questions? Class dismissed!" On the one hand, the action appears to maximize utility. No one has to work and no one is hurt. On the other hand, consider that the students are nursing students who need to learn the class material in order to function as competent nurses. If they do not learn the material, it is easy to see that they will be incompetent nurses. A society of incompetent nurses decreases the net utility and therefore, in this case, cancelling class decreases net utility.

Note again how utilitarianism differs from egoism. If the teacher and the students were egoists, and would rather skip class than work, there would be no class. On the contrary, utilitarians assume that the net utility decreases if no teaching and learning take place. Remember, utilitarians usually prescribe exactly what other moral theories do. They forbid killing, lying, cheating, and stealing and prescribe helping others, working hard, and doing good deeds.

However, there are times when utilitarianism prescribes more controversial actions. Consider euthanasia. The natural law tradition, which has exerted more influence on Western ethics than any other, maintains that it is wrong to intentionally kill innocent persons even if they are suffering. But suppose Joe Smith is terminally ill, in excruciating pain, and asks his wife, his trusted comrade of fifty years, to shoot him. Since he is more affected by his illness than anyone else, it is reasonable to assume the net utility will increase by his death. There will be some unhappiness caused by his death--his wife will mourn--but she would rather he die than suffer.

According to the utilitarian, if his wife shoots him as he requests, she does the moral thing. This analysis applies whether he killed himself or had his physician assist him. Here is a case in which what many of us believe to be immoral is, on utilitarian analysis, perfectly acceptable. In this case, the pain and suffering of the relevant parties determines the proper course of action for a utilitarian.

Examine some other controversial cases. Many cultures have practiced infanticide, the willful killing of innocent children. Often their rationale was that the lack of available food for all children required that the youngest and most dependent be sacrificed for the group. On a utilitarian analysis, this is perfectly acceptable because one death is preferable to many. The same kind of thinking might have justified the use of atomic weapons in World War II. Assuming the choice was between "x" number of deaths as a result of dropping atomic bombs and "4x" number of deaths as a result of a land invasion of Japan by American troops, the utilitarian choice was clear.

If other options were available that had a greater net utility--say dropping the bomb in an unpopulated field as a show of force--then that action should have been performed. We may object that in the case of infanticide or atomic bombs, "innocence" has a moral significance which overrides the utilitarian conclusion. But, according to the utilitarian, maximizing utility determines the proper action.

4. Mill and Utilitarianism

John Stuart Mill, a protegee of Bentham and Mill's father James Mill, became the most eloquent spokesman for utilitarianism. Mill was one of the most fascinating individuals in the history of Western philosophy. A child prodigy, he studied Greek and mathematics from the age of three and read all of Plato's dialogues in Greek by his early teens. Mill's classic work, *Utilitarianism*, sets forth the major tenets of the doctrine and reformulates many of Bentham's ideas.

In Chapter 2 of *Utilitarianism*, Mill noted that utilitarianism had concentrated upon the quantity of pleasure but it did not address any qualitative differences in pleasure. Mill feared the emphasis on pleasure would reduce utilitarianism to hedonism, a doctrine he considered "worthy of swine." He argued that some pleasures are qualitatively better than others, that the "higher" mental pleasures are superior in quality to the "lower" physical pleasures. How do we know this? Those who have experienced both kinds of pleasure show a decided preference for the higher ones, Mill stated, and this demonstrates that the higher pleasures are preferable. But are they really?

Mill admitted that non-human animals sometimes appear happier than human beings, but this is misleading. To paraphrase his famous quote: better an unhappy human than a happy pig; better a dissatisfied Socrates than a satisfied fool. If the fool or pig disagree, Mill continued, it is only because they have not experienced higher pleasures. The major difficulty with Mill's view was its appeal to a standard other than happiness in order to make a distinction between kinds of happiness. But if there is another value besides happiness, then we have abandoned the idea that happiness is the only good.

In Chapter 4, Mill began by defining the desirable end of all human endeavors. The only thing desirable is happiness, and all other valuable things are only means to the end of happiness. Bentham had wavered as to whether happiness or pleasure was the only good. In this more lucid version, happiness replaced pleasure as *the* moral standard. In this way, Mill avoided the charge that utilitarianism is hedonism in disguise.

Mill then proceeded to offer his famous "proof" of utilitarianism. We prove that something is visible by the fact that people see it and we prove that something is audible by the fact that people hear it. In the same way "the sole evidence it is possible to produce that anything is desirable, is that people do actually desire it." For Mill, the simple fact that people desire happiness establishes it as desirable.

Of course merely because people desire happiness, the opponents of Mill replied, does not show that it is the *only* desirable thing. Mill answered that other goods like virtue or wealth are really means to happiness. But his opponents pointed to another difficulty with Mill's proof. It rests upon a confusion between what people do desire and what they ought to desire. There mere fact that people actually desire happiness does not show, so critics of utilitarianism maintained, that happiness really should be desired. But Mill maintained that no other proof of the desirability of happiness was possible than to point out the fact that humans naturally desire it.

Mill also makes it clear that only the consequences matter. You do the right thing--maximize utility--by saving your friends from drowning whether you do it for love or money. After all, the net utility is merely the sum of individual utilities, and if *you* are happy, all the better. Why, Mill wonders, should we do our duty if it makes us unhappy? Amarillo Slim, a famous professional poker player, expressed Mill's position succinctly when he replied to someone who criticized his occupation: "Would the world really be better off if I was miserable pumping gas?"

5. Act and Rule Utilitarianism

Let us now turn to the question of whether utilitarians consider individual actions or classes of actions when deciding to maximize utility. Neither Bentham or Mill addressed this question, but contemporary philosophers have made a distinction between two types of utilitarians. **Act utilitarians** ask "which individual action, from the available alternatives, maximizes utility?" **Rule utilitarians** ask "which rule, when generally adopted, maximizes utility?" Oftentimes there is no difference between the prescriptions of the two types of utilitarians; at other times, there is a great difference. We will illustrate this basic difference with a number of examples.

Imagine that we are stopped at a red traffic light at three in the morning. Looking both ways as far as possible down the road we are about to cross, we see no cars in sight. It suddenly occurs to us that we should not remain stopped. Why? Because by running the red light we will save our mother a minutes worry, the country a little gas and pollution, and ourselves a little annoyance. Furthermore, we will get home sooner rather than later, decreasing the possibility that we or others will be injured in an accident. The net utility will be increased by our action and so, according to an act utilitarian, we should do it.

Contemplate another example. The President has requested that we turn down our thermostats to save heating oil. Unfortunately, our grandmother's arthritis is aggravated by a cold apartment. We reason as follows: if grandother keeps her heat high, she will not contribute significantly to the country's oil problem. Moreover, she will feel much better and so will we. She will be more comfortable physically, and we will not have to listen to her complain about arthritis, government corruption, or greedy oil companies. Her physical state positively affects her mood. Her good mood makes us and our family happier. An act utilitarian advises grandmother to keep her heat on high.

Finally, ponder this simple case. The sign on the college lawn says "keep off the grass." Officials at the college have determined that the college looks better, and attracts more students, with nice lawns. Now suppose you are in a hurry to complete some task that will make you *and others* happier, assuming that you complete it sooner rather than later. Assume also that cutting across the lawn saves a significant amount of time. Again, act utilitarians reason that their little footprints do not make a significant difference in the appearance of the college lawn, and since we can make so many other people happy by cutting across the lawn and completing our task sooner rather than later, we should do so.

Now consider these three cases from a rule utilitarian perspective. In every case the rule utilitarian asks, "what if we made a general rule of these actions?" In other words, "what if everybody did these?" (This is the Kantian question, but Kant wants to know about the consistency, not the consequences, of rules.) Rule utilitarians want to know if rules maximize utility or bring about good consequences. Take the first case. It should be clear that if everyone disobeys traffic lights the consequences are disastrous. Given the choice between a rule that states "always obey traffic lights" or one that says "sometimes obey traffic lights," the first rule, not the second one, maximizes utility. Rule utilitarians argue that the net utility will decrease if persons are more selective about their obedience to rules. They might begin to disobey traffic lights at 11 p.m., whenever there are no cars in sight, or *whenever they think they can beat the oncoming cars*!

A comparable analysis applies in the other two case. The rule, "do not turn up your thermostat to save heat for the country" maximizes utility compared with the rule, "turn up your thermostat if your are cold despite what the President requests." Similarly, the rule "do not walk on the grass" maximizes utility compared with the rule, "do not walk on the grass except when you are in a hurry." Therefore, in all of these cases act and rule utilitarians prescribe different actions. Act utilitarians perform the action that maximizes the utility, rule utilitarians act in accordance with the rule that, when generally adopted, maximizes utility. They both believe in maximizing utility but are divided as to whether the principle of utility applies to individual acts or general rules.

The issue between act and rule utilitarians revolves around the question, "is the moral life improved by practicing selective obedience to moral rules?" The act utilitarians answer in the affirmative, the rule utilitarians in the reverse. Rule utilitarians believe the moral life depends upon moral rules without which the net utility decreases. Act utilitarians believe that whether moral rules are binding or not depends upon the situation. Thus, act utilitarians treat moral rules as mere "rules of thumb," general guidelines open to exceptions, while rule utilitarians regard moral rules as more definitive. We will look at problems for both formulations of utilitarians in a moment. Let us now look at the most general problems for utilitarianism.

6. The Problems with Happiness

A first difficulty with using happiness as *the* moral standard is that the concept of the net utility implies that happiness and unhappiness are *measurable* quantities. Otherwise, we cannot determine which actions produce the greatest net utility. Bentham elaborated a "hedonistic calculus" which measured different kinds of happiness and unhappiness according to their intensity, duration, purity, and so on. Some say that it is impossible to attach precise numerical values to different kinds of happiness and unhappiness. For example, it may be impossible to assign a numerical value to the happiness of eating ice cream compared to the happiness of reading Aristotle. Still, we can prefer one to the other, say ice cream to Aristotle, and, therefore, we do not need precise numerical calculations to reason as a utilitarian.

A second difficulty is that it may be impossible to have "interpersonal" comparisons of utility. Should we give Sue our Aristotle book or Sam our ice cream? Does Sue's reading pleasure exceed Sam's eating pleasure?

There is no doubt that different things make different people happy. For some, reading and learning is an immense joy, for others, it is an exceptional ordeal. But we can still maximize utility. We should give Sue the book *and* Sam the ice cream, or if we can only do one or the other, we make our best judgment as to which action maximizes utility. Besides, we agree about many of the things that makes us happy and unhappy. Everyone is happy with some wealth, health, friends, and knowledge. Everyone becomes unhappy when they are in pain, hungry, tired, thirsty, and the like. We do not need precise interpersonal comparisons of utility to reason as a utilitarian.

Despite Mill's proof of utilitarianism, a third difficulty concerns doubts about the overriding value of happiness. Is it more valuable than, for example, freedom or friendship? Would we sacrifice these for the net utility? We would maximize utility by dropping "happiness pills" into everyone's drinks, but this doesn't mean we should do it. Shouldn't individuals be free to be unhappy? And if we believe this, isn't that because we think freedom is a value independent of happiness? We might even refuse to take happiness pills even if given the choice, because they limit the freedom to be *unhappy*.

Or suppose we promise to meet a friend but, in the meantime, some little children ask us to play with them. It may be that playing with the children maximizes utility. After all, our friend is popular and will probably make other arrangements after waiting a while. But maybe we should keep our promise. Maybe promise-keeping or the friendship it engenders are valuable independent of the total happiness. These examples suggest that happiness is not the only value.

Most contemporary utilitarians have abandoned the idea that happiness is the only value. They have retreated from claims about absolute values to claims about individual preferences. (This was Gauthier's argument in Chapter 4.) The type of utilitarianism which argues that we should maximize an individual's subjective preferences is called *preference utilitarianism*. The problem with this type of utilitarianism is that some subjective preferences might be evil.

A fourth difficulty is that *utilitarianism considers only the quantity of utility not its distribution.* Should you give $100 to one needy person or $10 each to ten needy persons? The second alternative might be better even if the first one creates the most utility. Concerns with the total happiness have troubled many commentators and some have suggested that we consider the "average utility." But this version has problems too. Do we want a society where the average income is very high--say $1,000,000--but many people live in destitute poverty, or one where the average income is much lower--say $30,000--but no poverty exists? In fact, the idea of the welfare state assumes that money has a diminishing utility--it doesn't benefit the rich as much as the poor--and thus the enforced government transfer of money from the rich to the poor is justified. But isn't it possible that individuals who work hard for their money *deserve* it, whether or not forcefully taking it maximizes utility? This analysis reveals another fundamental difficulty with utilitarianism. Everything is sacrificed to the net utility. But should all moral acts be judged by the consequences they produce?

7. The Problem with Consequences

The most important difficulty for utilitarianism is that it emphasizes consequences exclusively. Utilitarians claim that "the ends always justify the means," and therefore we can do *anything* to maximize utility as long as the consequences are good. For example, imagine that our neighbor opens our mail every day before we get home and then meticulously closes and replaces it with such skill that we cannot tell it has been opened. He derives great satisfaction from this activity and we never find out about it. When we are out of town and give him the key for emergencies, he rummages through our mail and personal effects, carefully replacing them before we return. He finds these activities immensely pleasurable, we never find out, and the net utility increases. An act utilitarian says he acts morally. But isn't there something wrong here? Should our privacy be sacrificed to the net utility?

Act utilitarians are willing to sacrifice privacy, rights, or even life itself to the net utility. Imagine a country sheriff who has been charged with finding the perpetrator of a recent homicide. The powerful elite of the town inform the sheriff that if he does not find the murderer, they will kill the inhabitants of the local American-Indian reservation, since they believe an American-Indian committed the crime. The sheriff has no idea who committed the murder, but he does believe that framing some innocent individual will avert the ensuing riot which will almost certainly kill hundreds of innocent people. In other words, the sheriff maximizes utility by *framing an innocent victim.*

Now according to an act utilitarian, this analysis is certainly correct. Nonetheless, most individuals think something is terribly mistaken with framing innocent persons. But why? If we don't frame the innocent victim, hundreds of people will die. True, something may foul our plan. For example, someone may find out that the victim has been framed. But this just repeats a critique of utilitarianism--that we never know the consequences for certain--which we have already answered. All the sheriff can do is the best he can. That is all anybody can do. And remember, if we do not frame the innocent victim, the blood of hundreds of other innocent victims is on our hands.

This is a situation in which a moral theory conflicts with our moral intuition. We ordinarily assume we shouldn't frame innocent people. But maybe that is just *ordinarily*? And this is an extraordinary situation. Nevertheless, most of us think something is terribly wrong here. Maybe the theory can be reformulated to handle these cases?

8. The Problems with Rule Utilitarianism

Problems of this sort are precisely what led to the formulation of rule utilitarianism. Rule utilitarians claim that the rules "never violate a person's privacy" or "never frame innocent persons" maximize utility compared with the rules "sometimes violate a person's privacy" or "sometimes frame innocent persons." But rule utilitarianism is beset by its own unique difficulties.

A first problem is whether utilitarian rules allow exceptions. To illustrate, consider that the moral rule "never kill the innocent" maximizes utility compared to the rule "always kill the innocent," and thus a strict rule utilitarian adopts the former, from these two choices, without exceptions. But the rule "never kill the innocent except to save more innocent lives" might maximize the utility better than either of the other two rules. If it did, a strict rule utilitarian would adopt *it* without exceptions. But this is not the best possible rule either. The best possible rule is "never kill innocent people except when it maximizes the utility to do so." But if that is the best possible rule, *how is rule utilitarianism any different than act utilitarianism*?

The issue is further complicated by the fact that different interpretations of rule utilitarianism exist. In what we will call *a strong rule utilitarianism*, moral rules have no exceptions. In what we will call *a weak rule util-itarianism*, rules have some exceptions. The more exceptions we build into our moral rules, the weaker our version of rule utilitarianism becomes. But if we build enough exceptions into our moral rules, rule utilitarianism becomes indistinguishable from act utilitarianism.

Think about the traffic light again. A strict rule utilitarian says "do not go through traffic lights" because, compared with most other rules, this rule maximizes utility. If we compare it with the rules "go through traffic lights when you want to," or "go through traffic lights if you're pretty sure you won't cause an accident," it fares well. But compare it with the rule :"do not go through traffic lights except in situations where it maximizes the utility to do so." A rule utilitarian should find this rule acceptable because it is the best conceivable rule. But if rule utilitarians act according to this rule, then their theory is indistinguishable from act utilitarianism.

Strong rule utilitarians can avoid this problem by not allowing exceptions to rules. They argue that if we make exceptions in individual cases, then the net utility will decrease because individuals naturally tend to be bias because they make exceptions that favor themselves. The act utilitarians counter by calling rule utilitarians superstitious "rule-worshipers." If it maximizes the utility to do "x," then why obey a rule that prescribes "y?" This issue could be resolved with some modified rule utilitarianism that would allow exceptions but not collapse into the situational character of act utilitarianism. The attempt to formulate such rules completely has met with mixed success.

A second problem with rule utilitarianism is that it tells us to abide by the rules that maximize the utility *if generally accepted.* Suppose they aren't generally accepted? If we still abide by them we make useless sacrifices. Imagine that public television is conducting their annual fund-raising campaign. A rule utilitarian reasons that if everyone abides by the rule "give what you can to public television," the net utility will be increased. But suppose no one else contributes and public television goes broke? Then the individual that contributes has made a useless sacrifice. These objections show that many difficulties plague rule utilitarianism.

9. Conclusion

The two key concepts in utilitarian thinking--happiness and con-sequences--are problematic. Whereas deontology places moral value on something intrinsic to the agent--his/her intentions--utilitarianism places moral value on something extrinsic to the agent--the action's consequences in terms of happiness produced. For deontologists, the end never justifies the means; for utilitarians the end always justifies the means. Note that both theories are based on a principle. For Kant, the principle is the cate-gorical imperative and for Mill it is the principle of utility. The ultimate principle in natural law is to promote the good or natural and in contract theory it is to do what is in our own interest. But maybe all of these theories are too formal and precise. Is there any theory of moral obligation that is less reliant on objective, abstract, moral principles and more contingent upon subjective, concrete, human experience? It is to such a theory that we now turn.

Chapter 7

Existentialism

"When I consider the brief span of my life, swallowed up in the eternity before and after, the little space which I fill, and even can see, engulfed in the infinite immensity of spaces of which I am ignorant, and which know me not, I am frightened, and am astonished at being here rather than there; for there is no reason why here rather than there, now rather than then."
Blaise Pascal

1. Basic Ideas of Existentialism

Could it be that all of the major ethical theories discussed thus far are misguided? Aren't they all too precise and abstract to speak to an amorphous ethical reality? Kant believed that ethics could be completely formal while Aristotle thought that ethics could demand only limited precision. Perhaps no precision is possible in ethics at all. Existentialists believe that all of the major theories discussed thus far are mistaken--for precisely these reasons.

Existentialism is a philosophical movement whose origins are in the Danish philosopher Søren Kierkegaard (1813-1855). Other major figures in the movement include Friedrich Nietzsche (1844-1900), Karl Jaspers (1883-1969), Martin Heidegger (1899-1976), and Jean-Paul Sartre (1905-1980). Existential philosophy is incredibly rich and diverse, and its proponents include communists, socialists, atheists, theists, and nihilists. Despite this diversity, almost all existentialists share a few basic ideas that are relevant for our discussion.

Kierkegaard's rejection of a "rational and philosophical" Christianity serves as a starting point for our deliberation. He believed that Christianity erred by trying to be *reasonable*, when in fact it is based upon faith and trust. Faith is not a matter of affirming certain rational propositions, whether ethical or religious, but of acting in a certain way. Kierkegaard made this point in his famous retelling of the Biblical story of Abraham and his son Isaac. It was not reasonable for Abraham to sacrifice his son simply because God asked him to; instead, it was an act of faith. From an ethical point of view Abraham's action was immoral, but for Kierkegaard faith and religion transcend reason and ethics.

These considerations lead to the first basic idea of existentialism: *reason is an inadequate instrument with which to comprehend the values, depth, mystery, and meaning of life*. Reason's limitations were poignantly described by the Russian novelist Feodor Dostoyevsky: "...reason...satisfies [our] rational requirements. Desire, on the other hand, is the manifestation of life itself...And although when we're guided by our desires, life may turn into a messy affair, it's still life and not a series of square roots."

But as we saw in the first chapter, Western philosophy began when the Greeks used reason to understand the world. Plato thought that reason should rule the individual, and Aristotle believed that our rationality was the definitive characteristic of human nature. Greek rationalism led to a search for the rational and objective foundations of knowledge, meaning, truth, and value, and, to a large extent, this book has followed this search.

The existentialists reject this tradition. They repudiate the abstract, the obtuse, the specialized, the esoteric, and the formal subtlety which divorces the intellect from life. They maintain that life is not an equation or riddle to be rationally resolved. In Gabriel Marcel's (1889-1973) words: "life is not a problem to be solved, but a mystery to be lived." The inability of reason to provide ultimate explanations was made explicitly by Marcel: "Whatever its ultimate meaning, the universe into which we have been thrown cannot satisfy our reason--let us have the courage to admit it once and for all."

Existentialism emphasizes *concrete personal experience over rational abstractions*. This is its second basic idea. We can see this point clearly in Albert Camus' (1913-1960) novel *The Stranger*. Camus depicts a conversation between a Catholic priest and Meursault, the story's central character who is in prison and condemned to death. In response to the priest's assurance that there is an afterlife, Meursault answers, "none of his certainties was worth one strand of a woman's hair." The point is that theories, speculations, and metaphysical and moral abstractions are worth less than concrete reality.

The emphasis on the concrete is also captured in the existential dictum "existence precedes essence." This means that we exist first, as particular, concrete, human subjects before we are defined by any universal, objective form or essence. Existence refers to "that a thing is," while essence refers to "what a thing is." For instance, the essence of the four-legged, tail-wagging, car-chasing thing we have at home is "dogness." That is what it is! The existentialist deny that there is any "human nature" that tells us what we ought to do, rather, we exist first as concrete human subjects and then proceed to create our essence. Fate or God do not determine us, we determine ourselves. We may become saints or sinners, but it is up to us to decide. In the same way, moral theories--which are intellectual abstractions--cannot tell us what to do; they cannot decide ethical questions for concrete human subjects. Intellectual theories are too detached from life to provide any guidance in our concrete lives. Theories may provide the rationale for human actions, but they cannot command our assent.

We can see easily how moral theories cannot make us do anything. Whether natural law, a social contract, the categorical imperative, or the net utility describe the essence of morality, their prescriptions cannot command our conduct because we can always ask, "why follow these theories?" Moral theories may define our moral duties and obligations, but they mean nothing without *personal commitment*. Action "x" may violate the natural law, the social contract, the categorical imperative, and the greatest happiness principle but, "so what?" That doesn't tell us we shouldn't do "x." These theories all assume ethics is objective, that is, that some actions really are right or wrong. Against this objectivism, existentialism emphasizes the human subject as the only ultimate source of morality. Only when we commit ourselves to some course of action do we act as moral agents.

The emphasis on personal commitment brings us to a third basic idea of existentialism: *human beings are radically free*. We are the ones who create the meaning, truth, and value in our lives, and we are totally responsible for our lives. We often claim to be unable or powerless to do certain things, but, in fact, we don't do them because *we don't want to*. And if wanted to do them we would! For instance, the fact that it is wrong to steal doesn't prevent us from doing it, only *we* can do that. True, we cannot do everything--we cannot fly or be across the globe instantaneously--but we do choose from our available options and, in the process, create ourselves. In summary, existentialism claims that: Moral theories which derive from rational thinking are defective because *they emphasize personal abstraction over experience, and they cannot account for the role that human freedom--manifested by personal commitment--plays in the moral domain.*

2. Sartre And Freedom

Jean-Paul Sartre, the most famous existentialist of all, was a philosopher, playwright, political activist, and social critic. The complexities and nuances of his philosophy are formidable, but Sartre's philosophy best characterizes the unique features of an existential ethics. The key concepts in the Sartrian analysis of ethics are: freedom, angst, bad faith, and authenticity. We discuss each in turn.

We begin our discussion with Sartre's notion that *we are radically free*. If we are in a bad mood, for example, it is because we choose to be. The external world does not impose itself upon our consciousness, we control our moods, thoughts, attitudes, and choices. No better example of our control over external circumstance can be found than in the writings and life of Victor Frankl, who suffered in a concentration camp in World War II. Despite the horrendous conditions, he discovered that he was the master of his fate: "Ultimately, [we are] not subject to the conditions that confront [us]; rather, these conditions are subject to [our] decision...[we] must decide whether [we] will face up or give in, whether or not [we] will let [ourselves] be determined by the conditions."

And we are *not* determined by our past choices! As Frankl puts it, "all choices are caused but they are caused by the chooser." We can easily demonstrate. Suppose we are trying to decide whether to study or drink ten beers tonight. No theory or promise eliminates this choice. Early in the morning we might say to ourselves, "tonight I will forego the beer and study." But when the evening comes we must make a choice, beer or books! Or suppose we promise ourselves that on Monday we will start a new diet. But when Monday comes, our former promise means nothing. At that moment we must decide, diet or dessert? Our promises, ideals, and theories mean nothing because, when the moment of choice arrives, we stand face to face with human freedom. In the same way our past promises do not determine our present choices, our present choices do not determine the future. We may want to be great writers, but *nothing we say now determines the future*. No matter how we try to deny our freedom, it forces itself upon us.

For Sartre, freedom derives from human consciousness. We are conscious of both objects in the world and of ourselves as subjects, and this self-consciousness is the source of freedom. Self-conscious beings can imagine themselves as more muscular, attractive, knowledgeable, spiritual, famous, or wealthy. In short, they can be conscious of what they lack, and can freely choose to fill these voids. Thus, freedom emanates from our consciousness of possibilities, particularly the possibility that we can be more than we are now. The concept of freedom is difficult to conceptualize and articulate precisely because, if Sartre is correct, it is not an abstraction. Rather, it is intensely experienced in the moment of our actual, concrete choices.

Unfortunately, freedom is paradoxical. In the first place, we are free to do anything except not make choices, we cannot *not* be free. We are, in Sartre's words, "condemned to be free." This frightening phrase captures the essence of the paradox of freedom. *We cannot escape freedom*! To illustrate, suppose that we want to know if we should perform active euthanasia on our terminally ill parent. We can choose to do it or not, *but we cannot not choose*! There is no escape from the fact that humans stand alone in the world and choose, and this realization reveals how freedom is not a blessing.

Consider another example. We are trying to choose between believing or disbelieving in the existence of the Judeo-Christian God. We can choose to believe, to not to believe, or to hold our belief in abeyance. But any choice carries with it an awesome responsibility. If we believe because we think it is the safest choice or because we have been told, we are responsible for our pragmatism or credulity. If we do not believe because we have no evidence or because we do not care, we are responsible for our skepticism or apathy. And if we do not choose either, we are responsible for our indecision. Furthermore, making no choice is a choice itself. Thus, though all choices carry risk, *we cannot not make them.*

One way to try to escape our freedom is to accept creeds and theories which tell us what acts must be performed. But this does not solve the problem. We have simply taken the choice to another level where the question becomes, "what creeds should we subscribe to?" There is no escape from the fact that *we are prisoners of freedom*. Sartre summed up his views on freedom in his famous public lecture in Paris on October 29, 1945: "Thus we have neither behind us, nor before us, in a luminous realm of values, any means of justification or excuse. We are left alone, without excuse. That is what I mean when I say that [humans are] condemned to be free."

3. Angst and Bad Faith

According to Sartre, when we encounter freedom and realize its paradox, we experience **angst** or anxiety. This anxiety results from the grave difficulty we have in accepting total responsibility for our acts. We are alone in the world without any guidance or any eternal principles to inform and console us. Instead, we must create our own values; we are like Gods! As Sartre puts it: "To be [human] means to reach towards being God. Or if you prefer, [humanity] fundamentally is the desire to be God." We experience the dread of knowing we can do *anything*. But angst, anxiety, or dread result from the complete responsibility that accompanies our freedom to create value.

So great is freedom and its accompanying angst, that it is easier to deny freedom by avoiding painful decisions and pretending that freedom does not exist. Sartre says there are three ways this can be done. The first is to fail to choose. But, as we have just seen, to not choose is a choice itself, thus, non-choice does not allow one to escape from freedom. The second is to be what Sartre calls a "serious-minded" individual who pretends that some objective values dictate the right choice to them. But as Kierkegaard pointed out, these values mean nothing unless we make them our own. They cannot make us do anything.

Sartre's demonstrated how moral values fail in the example of the young man who must decide whether to stay home with his mother or go off to join the French Free forces fighting the Germans in World War II. His father had collaborated with the Nazis, but his brother had been killed trying to stop the German offensive in 1940. The young man wanted to avenge his brother's death, but his mother was alone and wanted him to stay in France. What should the young man do?

Sartre claimed that no moral theory could resolve this dilemma. It does not help to claim that the young man should do his duty, since he experiences a conflict of duties. It doesn't help to recommend that he should do the good or the natural, inasmuch as he cannot ascertain what the good or natural is. It is no help to follow the principle of utility either, because he does not know what might happen. He might stay home and feel guilty or go to war and be killed. He cannot even be sure what is in his own interest! Sartre asserts that the young man must choose a course of action by himself and live with complete responsibility for the consequences. Abstract theories fail in real life situations, Sartre says, because real life is not an esoteric puzzle. Life is about flesh and blood, men and women, and life and death.

The third and most important way to deny freedom is to act in **bad faith**. We act *unauthentically* or in bad faith by thinking of ourselves as passive objects manipulated by other people, social conventions, religious commands, or moral codes. In other words, *we deny our subjectivity*! Sartre tells the story of a young woman who is being slowly seduced. As the young man's hand begins to touch her, she pretends not to notice. She believes that something is happening *to her*, that she is a passive object. But this is mistaken! She is allowing it to happen and can stop the young man, but she acts in bad faith by pretending not to be free. Or consider students who do not want to read and study and who blame the teacher or school for their failure. They are mistaken; they could study hard. When we avoid painful decisions and pretend that we are not free, we are acting in *bad faith*; we are refusing to take responsibility for our actions.

In perhaps his most famous example of bad faith, Sartre tells the story of a waiter who thinks of himself as an object controlled by the role he plays. He denies his freedom to leave at anytime, to just walk out! He is not controlled by the role, the rules, the society, moral theory, God, or anything else. He can be what he wants, even if that means becoming unemployed and living on the streets. But the awesome nature of this responsibility invites a retreat from freedom and exemplifies bad faith.

Our actions--not ethical theories or abstract principles--create value. Unauthentic individuals act in bad faith by pretending that they cannot freely create value. Bad faith reveals itself not only in specific situations, but in a general attitude toward life. The Protestant theologian Paul Tillich (1886-1965) put the matter like this: "Existential anxiety of doubt drives the person toward the creation of certitude of systems of meaning, which are supported by tradition and authority. Neurotic anxiety builds a narrow castle of certitude which can be defended with the utmost tenacity." We reduce anxiety by accepting systems, theories, and principles that give certitude. But in so doing, we fail to ask questions and, in this way, we do not actualize our potential to doubt and thereby be fully human. We refuse to search for the values that make life meaningful and do not confront with courage the anxiety that accompanies the creation of value in our own lives. In Tillich's words, we do not have "the courage to be."

4. Authenticity

If we have the courage to *be*, the courage to create value, the courage to commit to a course of action and accept full responsibility for our choices, we act **authentically** or in good faith. Sartre does not say much about good faith except that it involves choosing the values, purposes, and projects for which we take full responsibility. Authentic individuals do not allow anything to dictate to them, they simply choose to *commit themselves* to a particular course of action.

But is there nothing more to say about morality than that we should freely choose a course of action? If nothing, not even God, can be a source of value then this is all Sartre can say, and he *did* claim that there are no values without conscious beings. Sartre did make one attempt to ground his ethics on something other than freedom. In "Existentialism Is a Humanism," he compared the existential value of freedom with the value humanism places on universal freedom. But this runs counter to his general claim that we try to overcome the other's freedom, and, for the most part, commentators have rejected the view that existentialism is a humanism.

Thus, it seems impossible for there to be any existential ethics for conscious beings. For, where would these values come from? Conscious beings do know the objects of the world, but the realm of facts is devoid of values. Furthermore, nothing that destroys the absolute freedom of self-conscious beings can be the source of values. If there were objective values, Sartre argued, humans would not be totally free to create their own values. Thus, there is no foundation for my nature or my actions, for if there were, my freedom would be limited. There cannot be any non-relative, non-temporal, immutable, absolute, or objective moral truths for Sartre, and therefore moral truth is subjective. We now turn to some difficulties for an existential ethics.

5. Does Freedom Exist?

In Chapter 2 we concluded that determinism did not negate human freedom. But what is the extent of our freedom? We might consider some specific limitations on human freedom in order to determine its extent.

First, our freedom of action may be limited. Someone can put a gun to our head and tell us not to move, or the law may decree that we not drive 100 miles per hour. In the strictest sense, we still have some freedom in these cases, since we can move despite our assailant's gun or drive fast regardless of the police radar. But some options have been removed. We cannot move without there being a chance of getting shot or drive fast without the chance of getting caught!

Second, our freedom of choice may be restricted. If we do not have the money to vacation on the Riviera or if we do not know that Tahiti is an island in the South Pacific, then we are hardly free to go to either place. In the strictest sense, we still have some freedom in these cases too. We can take an extra job to save for vacation or read travel magazines about south sea travel options. But we are not free to go to either place without increasing either our wealth or knowledge.

Third, our freedom to deliberate rationally may be impeded. If we are drunk, we have lost most of our ability to make rational choices, and if we are comatose or in a persistent vegetative state, our freedom to deliberate is completely absent. Perhaps even worse, our freedom to live, breathe, love, and rationally deliberate can be erased by an assassin's bullet. Unforeseen circumstances can eliminate both our ability to rationally deliberate and the freedom that goes with it. In sum, freedom is not unlimited.

Despite all of the possible limitations on our freedom, we may still affirm freedom's existence. Although basketball players cannot literally fly through the air, they exercise great freedom within the limits set by their physical capabilities and the rules of the game. Still the critics reply, freedom ultimately can be denied. Frankl's valiant effort to the contrary, many of us could be forced to repudiate our freedom in difficult circumstances. When confronted with his worst fear, Winston Smith, the central character in George Orwell's *1984*, turns on his beloved to avoid his own gruesome fate.

In Orwell's story the government controls through propaganda, censorship, and persuasion. But we could imagine an even worse scenario. Imagine that a government put something in our water which would eradicate our ability to deliberate rationally. In that case, our freedom would be erased. In fact, assuming they had not stored enough untainted water to last a lifetime, even the government officials would lose their freedom.

On the other hand, these stories may exemplify freedom. Winston *did not have to turn on his beloved*! He had to choose whether the gruesome fate would befall him or his beloved, and he chose her! And, in our "thought experiment" about a corrupt government, Sartre would probably maintain that some of us freely choose to abolish freedom, supporting his claim that we are free. If we decide that freedom is no longer a value, then we might choose to eliminate it. Thus, though the existentialists may have exaggerated the extent of our freedom, they are right to make it a significant part of morality. In the moral arena we *experience* freedom all the time.

Finally, we might consider briefly Marcel's view that freedom is not something given, but something earned. We are not *born* free, freedom is not an attribute, and, thus, some individuals are more free than others. We must make ourselves free or, as Marcel puts it: "freedom is a conquest--always partial, always precarious, always challenged." We must struggle to free ourselves from external conditions and subjective limitations. But to do this, Marcel says, we need hope: "the freest [person] is the one who has the most hope." If we hope, we are open to permanent alteration, open to overcoming our limitations. "Insofar as I hope, I release myself from an inner determinism comparable to a cramp." Hope alleviates the despair that results from the belief that we are determined. In our hope for future possibilities, we open the future to the possibility of being altered by our freedom. We act in good faith.

6. Good Faith And Bad

When acting in bad faith, we pretend that something controls our behavior. Imagine individuals who live according to the moral principles with which they have been raised. Occasionally, they have considered that these principles may be groundless and that they could reject them. However, the idea that they can create their own principles, values, and meaning in life is frightening. The moment any doubt appears in their minds, they cease thinking. Instead of pondering their choices, they simply accept the values with which they have been raised.

Sartre believes such individuals are morally culpable for accepting as binding their initial moral principles. Furthermore, they act in bad faith when they deny their freedom and suppose that these principles control them. But are such individuals really so bad? Suppose they are pleasant, dutiful, conscientious, and kind? Against Sartre, we argue that the mere fact that these individuals deceive themselves into thinking they are controlled by moral rules, or have never considered the possibility of other principles, does not make them immoral.

Now our appraisal would probably be different if these individuals had just "accepted" more dubious principles. If they had been taught since youth to torture animals and set houses on fire, we would likely condemn the actions that follow from their principles in the same way we condemn individuals who just "follow orders." But this suggests that we condemn them, not because they act in bad faith, but because their principles and actions are immoral. In the case of harmless simpletons, we were hesitant to condemn them because *they did nothing wrong*! In the case of cruel individuals, we condemn both them because *they did do something wrong!* This suggests that it doesn't matter whether actions are done in good or bad faith, but whether the actions are good or bad. Does the mere fact that we act in good or bad faith really matter?

The point becomes even clearer if we examine cases of actions done in good faith. Imagine individuals who strive all of their life to create their own values. After a long and arduous intellectual journey, they decide that there is no God or objective values; nonetheless, they dedicate their lives to working arduously in cancer research. They give no reason for this choice other than to say, "we freely commit ourselves to this project and take full responsibility for the outcome of our life." Whatever else we may think of it, there is something praiseworthy about this enterprise, this life lived in good faith.

This exemplifies what some existentialists call a *project*. Projects are self-created endeavors which allow us to experience freedom and authenticity. Whether our project is to be mother, father, medical researcher, doctor, teacher, dancer, or concert pianist, the way we do it, according to Sartre, says more about the morality of the action than the action itself. This follows from the fact that there are no objective values, only subjective motives, intentions, feelings, and emotions that we bring to our choices. If we act in good faith--the unique expression of our own being with full recognition of our freedom and its attached responsibility--then we act morally.

The problem here is with sincere killers or Nazis. If they really believe they are doing the right thing--say killing for God--and do it without hypocrisy and in good faith then, according to the existentialists, they act morally. And it doesn't matter what they do, they are moral if they act in good faith. Here we encounter the same problems that plagued other therise of subjective value. If there is no objective foundation to morality, then anything is allowable. Thus, good and bad faith are unable to distinguish between what we ordinarily assume are right and wrong actions. This sungents that something more is needed to understand the nature of morality. But is it possible for an existentialist to avoid the Sartrian conclusion that ethics is nothing more than making choices in good faith?

7. Other Existential Thinkers

One of the ways to avoid Sartre's conclusion is to rely upon God as the ultimate source of objective value. For Kierkegaard, ethical principles have their place, but they are subservient to God who can suspend them. God does not always share our moral judgments or the dictates of our moral conscience. If that were the case, we would only need our conscience, in order to be moral, and would not need God. According to Kierkegaard's philosophy, faith is higher than reason in the moral domain, inasmuch as moral principles and theological abstractions mean nothing without an intensely personal commitment to the moral or religious way of life.

Other religious existentialists like Marcel and Tillich have taken up the Kierkegaardian project. In one way or another, they have rejected proofs for the existence of God and absolute moral principles. Like Sartre, they all emphasize human subjects and their freedom, but unlike Sartre, they accept God as the source of objective value. Thus, a religious existential ethics rejects the rationalism of natural law ethics and, at least in Kierkegaard's case, moves in the direction of a divine command theory. However, by positing an objective source for morality, ethics may more properly be called religious than existential. As such, it is open to all of the philosophical objections we may pose for any religious claim. We may still ask, "why should we believe?" Thus, a theological existentialism must be built upon a theology with all its attendant philosophical difficulties.

Another existentialist who tried valiantly to respond to the criticisms of existential ethics was the French writer Simone de Beauvoir (1908-1986). Like Sartre, de Beauvoir made freedom central to her ethics. In *The Ethics of Ambiguity*, she argued that we recognize the lack or the emptiness in our being and try to fill these spaces by freely choosing "projects." Projects are labors that disclose our own being. By engaging in a project, we experience the freedom to give our lives value and meaning. In the struggle to overcome the obstacles inherent in our project, we discover our own being as "free being."

De Beauvoir admits that ethics is ambiguous but not that it is absurd. If life were absurd, as Sartre contended, then nihilism would result. But amidst ambiguity, we have the opportunity to give life value and meaning. If values were translucent, we would not have this chance to disclose ourselves as free being through our projects. Since values are more opaque than translucent, the genuinely moral person "resides in the painfulness of an indefinite questioning." Ambiguity provides the field as it were in which we may create our values.

In the final analysis, freedom was the ultimate value for de Beauvoir, and she opposed any action that limited human freedom. The ultimate precept is "to treat...other[s]...as a freedom so that [their] end may be freedom." She gave the following example of how the precept worked. If others attempt suicide under the influence of intoxicants or temporary depression, we may interfere with their freedom. But if they want to end or ruin their lives after rational deliberation, we should allow them to do so. Despite her claim to the contrary, it seems unlikely that freedom is the only value or even the most important one. For example, most people do not think that freedom is more important than justice or life itself. In addition, whenever principles other than freedom are introduced, we move away from the spirit of an existential ethics. This is not to say that freedom cannot function as the ultimate moral principle, only that if it does we have another objective moral theory.

8. An Assessment

If we really do create values by freely choosing projects, then there is no way to distinguish good projects or actions from bad ones, other than to say some are freely chosen and some are not. But it just doesn't seem true that our commitment to something makes it valuable. Nor does it seem true that our lack of commitment makes something worthless. As with various elements of other theories we have examined, there is something counterintuitive about existential ethics. Thus, it appears there is something wrong with the existential account of value; it is too subjective.

Another difficulty with the existential theory of value is its irrationalism. If ethics is merely a matter of choosing, then no choice is irrational. If we ask existentialists why they chose "x," their only possible reply is, "we just choose." But this is unsatisfactory. If we can give no reason why we choose something, then our choice is not rational. In fact, existentialists can give no reason why they chose anything precisely because there is no reason to choose. If there were, then ethics would be rational and objective. This is another problem with the existential account of value; it is too irrational.

Of course an existentialist would reject this critique. They argue that the whole point of an existential ethic is to show that reason is an inadequate instrument to understand morality. But are we really satisfied with a theory that can give us no reason whatsoever why we ought to do something? If I tell you that you should go jump in the lake but cannot tell you why, aren't you hesitant to do it? And doesn't this show that reason must play *some* role in ethics? Thus, even if the existentialists are right about reason's limitations, it does not follow that reason plays no role in the moral sphere.

Other existentialists try to overcome the subjectivism and irrationalism with God, freedom, or some other objective standard. But this undermines the radical nature of existentialism, suggesting that the tedium of ethical theorizing is necessary to uncover the objective foundations of morality. Remember, existentialism was attractive because it proposed to bypass the arduous task of uncovering the principles operative in the moral arena, but without principles, existential ethics is bankrupt. The existentialists are correct when they argue that morality involves personal commitment, but if they cannot tell us what to be committed to or why, the theory is seriously deficient. If we reject existentialism, are there any other possibilities we have not considered?

Chapter 8

Contemporary Theories

"As a rule we disbelieve all facts and theories for which we have no use."
    William James

1. Introduction

So far our discussion has touched upon some of the most prominent ethical theories in Western intellectual history, but it has not exhausted the possibilities of ethical theory. There are a number of other theories which enjoy contemporary prominence. One of the theories we will discuss has its roots in antiquity, another in the seventeenth century, and the others are relatively recent. But all of these theories exemplify the continual quest for, and unending discussion about, philosophical truth. Let us address each of them in turn.

2. John Locke and Natural Rights

It is nearly impossible to be a citizen of the contemporary Western world without having encountered the idea that morality focuses upon **rights**. As opposed to the social nature of humanity emphasized by natural law theorists, natural rights theorists place prominence on *individual liberty*. Human freedom, they argue, exists naturally before legal and political institutions intervene, and only the consent of free individuals--a social contract--political power.

Modern theories of natural rights originated in seventeenth-century England with the philosopher John Locke. Throughout Locke's life, England was embroiled in a turbulent political debate that ultimately led to revolution. The main issue was *the divine right of kings*, the notion that the king received his authority from God. Locke defended those who supported parliamentary government, against the forces loyal to the Crown, in a conflict which culminated with the beheading of Charles I in 1649. The radical element of the revolutionary movement did not allow elections and installed Oliver Cromwell as virtual dictator. (Supporting the thesis of historian Will Durant that revolutionaries, when they assume power, are every bit as corrupt as those they have overthrown.)

Cromwell died in 1658 and was succeeded by his son Richard; Richard was weak and his ineptitude had much to do with the change in climate which led to the restoration of monarchy in 1660. Charles II then assumed power and ruled until his death in 1658 when his brother James II became king. A battle ensued between the Tories, who defended the monarchy, and the Whigs, who supported parliamentary government. James was driven from power and William and Mary assumed the throne, ruling jointly until 1688. However, William and Mary were forced to accept the English "Bill of Rights," which defined the individual's rights against governmental authority.

Throughout this tumultuous period, Locke defended the revolutionary elements in English society. His political theory championed one of the most influential ideas in modern history: *that all human beings have rights that no government may justifiably eliminate*. The violation of natural rights constituted sufficient justification for political revolution. According to Thomas Jefferson's interpretation, Locke's political theory justified the American revolution, and the American Declaration of Independence embodies many of the salient ideas of Locke's moral and political theory. Locke was, without a doubt, the chief philosophical inspiration of the creation of the American government. (His portrait hangs in Thomas Jefferson's study at Monticello.)

Locke's conception of the state of nature differed from Hobbes' understanding of it. Locke believed that a natural morality existed in the state of nature but because enforcement is impractical, government was created. Natural morality consists of individual rights which cannot legitimately be taken away by governments. According to Locke, the most prominent rights are *life, liberty, and property*. In contrast to Hobbes' view, the social order was not formed merely to preserve our lives but to *protect our rights*. The seeds of modern democracy can be found in Locke's contention that in a state of nature all individuals are "*morally free, equal, and independent.*"

It is important to note that this is a *moral* freedom and equality, since Locke certainly recognized that we are not physically or intellectually free and equal. Since all human beings have a right to moral freedom and equality, government has an obligation to respect the moral law embodied in natural human rights. Locke was indebted to the natural law tradition he had inherited because, like the natural law theorists, he believed the moral law can be known by human reason.

According to the natural rights theory, right conduct respects individual rights regardless of whether doing so promotes the individual or social good. Individuals have the right to live as they please without any duties to themselves or others as long as they respect the *rights* of others. Traditionally, rights theorists like Locke emphasized so-called *negative rights*: the right not to be killed, not to be denied liberty, not to have one's property forcefully seized. Government is limited by individual rights and exists solely to protect them. It should not interfere in our lives! Therefore, government's role is not to make us happy, virtuous, knowledgeable, or wealthy--it exists solely to protect our rights. Nonetheless, modern rights theorists have placed increasing emphasis on *positive rights*: the right to education, a decent standard of living, and health care. On this account, government must do much more than not interfere, it must actively help us achieve certain ends.

In the language of philosophical ethics, natural rights theory is deontological rather than teleological. We have no moral responsibility to promote human flourishing or maximize the net utility; in fact, we do not need to promote any values whatsoever! Instead, we should simply do our duty, which is to respect the boundaries of all person's *inalienable* rights.

3. Difficulties with Rights

In our own society, moral disagreements are often framed in terms of rights. We talk of the right to our lives, privacy, firearms, and pornography, just to name a few, and we grumble about "infringements" of our rights. Nonetheless, there are numerous philosophical questions about rights. How many rights do we have? What is a right? How do we determine what sorts of things have rights? How do we resolve cases in which rights conflict? Where do rights come from?

The *number* of rights advocated has increased incrementally over the past few centuries. Compare, for example, Locke's three basic rights with the thirty advocated by the United Nations Universal Declaration of Human Rights in 1948. It is not clear, even among rights theorists, how many rights we have. There is also little agreement about the *nature* of a right, and no universally acceptable way to adjudicate between disputant's claims concerning either the number or nature of rights.

In addition, to whom or what do rights apply? Do they apply to fetuses? To newborns? To mentally incompetents? To serial killers? To non-human animals? To intelligent aliens? To future generations? Rights were initially conceived as distinctively human, but they have been applied increasingly to non-human animals, ecosystems, planets, and the universe itself. Also, some claim that rights apply beyond single lifetimes to "possible" people! For example, that future generations have a right to a clean environment even though these individuals are not as yet actual? On the one hand it appears they do, but, on the other hand, the idea that a non-existent thing has rights is strange indeed. There is nothing in rights theory itself that allows us to determine what has rights.

Conflicts between competing rights are particularly intractable. If moral theory is unable to resolve these conflicts, then violence or moral mediation must settle the conflict. The only way to avoid this difficulty would be to prioritize rights. But can we really say that right #1 always takes precedence over right #2? And no priority of rights is complete without considering to which things rights apply.

And where do rights come from? Here, there are two competing schools of thought. The one argues that legal rights *precede* moral rights, that nothing is moral or immoral antecedent to the law. Thus, *moral rights come from our legal and political agreements; they come from us*. Furthermore, according to this view, any appeal to rights other than legal ones is in fact a disguised appeal to subjective values. When we say we have a natural moral right to "x" *independent* of the law, what we really mean is that we value "x."

The other view is that moral rights *precede* legal ones and that morality exists independently of the law. Thus, *moral rights come from the natural moral law; they come from something besides ourselves*. Furthermore, the natural moral law and the rights that stem from it can be known to rational human beings because they are self-evident. In the language of the constitution of the United States: "We hold these truths to be self-evident: That all men are created equal; that they are endowed by their Creator with certain inalienable rights; that among these are life, liberty, and the pursuit of happiness..."

But is it really *self-evident* that individuals have "inalienable" rights? Despite what the Founding Fathers say, this is not *philosophically* self-evident to us all. Thus, rights theory may enlighten the moral domain, but it comes nowhere close to resolving our difficulties. Maybe ethics should be more concerned with moral character than universal rights.

4. Virtue Ethics

Greek ethics differed from any of the theories we have discussed thus far. The Greeks were primarily interested in the question, "what character traits help individuals live good lives?" **Virtue ethics**, a contemporary moral theory whose genesis is in Aristotle, has turned our attention back toward questions about moral character. Our character, what today we call our personality, is the sum total of our habitual actions, and a *good* moral character is one filled with virtue. Aristotle's moral theory contemplated the nature of the virtuous or moral person. He was interested in what kind of moral character we possess, rather than what kind of principles we recommend. His moral theory does not offer a principle of utility or a categorical imperative to guide our conduct; instead, it tells us what kind of people we should be. In short, we should be persons of good moral character.

Modern philosophical ethics, beginning with Hobbes and continuing in the moral philosophies of Kant and Mill, has largely abandoned the Aristotelian approach. Modern philosophy has sought, at least since the sixteenth century, to formulate the rules and principle of morally obligatory actions. It has found the moral law variously in the social contract, human rationality, or net utility. As difficulties with determining specific moral rules and obligations plagued philosophy into the second half of the twentieth century, a return to an ethics of virtue was suggested. Why don't we relinquish the idea that moral philosophy can formalize the principles of the morality and focus instead upon moral character?

The key idea in virtue ethics is the concept of moral virtue. *A moral virtue is a character trait displayed habitually in human action which aids an individual in living well.* What counts as a virtue and which virtues are important is controversial; nonetheless, representative examples include: courage, justice, moderation, tolerance, honesty, fidelity, self-discipline, friendliness, cooperativeness, conscientiousness, loyalty, and industriousness. These virtues aid us in the pursuit of good and happy lives. For instance, courage is necessary to engage the world in a meaningful way, industriousness for a productive life, and honest, fidelity, and loyalty to have worthwhile friendships.

The role that other virtues play in *our* good life is more problematic. For example, justice seems to contribute to other's good lives more than our own. Both Plato and Aristotle believed that "other-regarding" virtues contribute to a good life to the extent that they shape a person's moral character. They argued that persons of bad moral character cannot have good lives. Specifically, Plato believed that unjust individuals--those without moral virtue--possess "disharmonious" souls, and Aristotle believed that the unjust are not capable of "virtue friendships." For most Greek thinkers the moral life and the happy life coincide.

The return to an ethics of virtue has a number of advantages. In the first place, its emphasis on personal transformation and moral character strikes a resounding chord. We have all encountered the gap between theory and practice revealed in human conduct. How many of us have known individuals who publicly proclaim but privately disregard moral principles? As the existentialists pointed out, principles cannot command us, we must rule ourselves. Virtuous individuals habitually perform moral actions.

Furthermore, a return to a virtue ethics has a number of societal advantages. If we could inculcate virtue in members of society, we would all benefit immensely. And, despite some disagreement concerning the importance of particular virtues, individuals from diverse ethnic and cultural backgrounds all regard certain virtues like honesty, loyalty, and self-discipline as important. The emphasis on moral character, instead of moral principles or individual autonomy, is the greatest strength of a virtue approach.

5. Difficulties with Virtue Ethics

As with all theories, there are a number of difficulties with virtue ethics. Its emphasis on moral character rectifies the deficiencies of theories that focus exclusively on moral principles or individual autonomy, but by omitting moral principles it fails to supply the means to resolve moral dilemmas. In other words, if we aren't sure what we should do in a particular moral dilemma, it does us no good to be told, "develop a good character!" Of course, the virtue ethician could say that right actions simply emanate from good moral characters, but it is hard to see what this would mean without some conception of moral principles upon which to act. Moral actions do not necessarily proceed from virtuous persons because virtuous individuals might be mistaken about what is right! In other words, we don't always "do the right thing" because we are good people.

A second difficulty relates to the inability of the virtue ethician to give us reasons to act. Other theories have given us these reasons: it maximizes utility, is in our self-interest, abides by the natural law, and so on. But why should we be honest according to the virtue approach? The only plausible answer seems to be because its virtuous to do so. But this "begs the question." It is empty to say that we should be virtuous because it is virtuous. Any reason to act virtuously must appeal to some other standard like self-interest or rationality or it cannot justify its own moral standard. (Unless we take an existentialist approach and simply choose virtue without reason.) Thus, by itself, virtue ethics is deficient. Having a good moral character, while certainly important in ethics, does not seem to settle all of our questions.

6. Feminist Ethics

A **feminist** is an individual who believes in the essential equality of women and men. Some feminists claim that only women can be feminists-- men sympathetic to their plight are called "profeminists"--while others accept that both men and women can be feminists. Recently, an issue related to our discussion has arisen within feminist philosophy: *the idea that traditional ethical philosophy includes a male bias.* We might understand this idea if we consider the following. Males have traditionally operated in the public arena of business, politics, and religion where contracts, laws, and principles reign. Women, on the other hand, have traditionally lived in the private world of the home where caring, cooperation, and love prevail. Reflecting these various experiences, traditional (male) moral theories, the critics argue, highlight contracts, law, duties, and principles *at the expense of* care, concern, cooperation, and love.

Some evidence suggests that these differences are deeply rooted in males and females. The educational psychologist Carol Gilligan argues that there are significant differences in how little girls and boys approach games. Basically, boys are interested in the "rules of the game" and will continue to play even when disagreements arise over the rules. Girls, on the other hand, are much less interested in the rules and more likely to quit playing when conflict over rules occur. It is easy to imagine that these basic differences recur in the way adult women and men approach ethics.

Another way traditional ethics incorporates a male bias is by emphasizing a disinterested, impartial rationality, the so-called "male voice." According to the critics, this "masculine" approach omits valuable components from the ethical dialogue; in particular, it overlooks the "female voice" which emphasizes intuition and emotion.

This distinction has led some philosophers to argue for a *feminist epistemology*, which contends that men and women possess different "ways of knowing." Some argue that women's ways of knowing are superior to men's, others that they are incompatible, and still others that they merely need to be combined, merged, or blended. Whatever the relationship between the two kinds of knowing, all feminist epistemologists argue that by including emotions and intuitions with logic and rationality we attain a superior picture of reality. If women's intellectual development assimilates the intuitive and emotional in determining truth and making value judgments and if these components have been absent in traditional ethical theorizing, then classic ethical theory is incomplete.

If men and women have customarily operated in different spheres and speak with different moral "voices," then there should be significant differences in the way they conceive the task of moral philosophy. All of these differences may be summarized under the rubrics of an *ethics of care* and an *ethics of justice*. The former stressing care, concern, responsibility, and relationships is the female voice; the latter featuring rules, rights, principles, and contracts is the male voice. The ethics of care depends upon intuition, emotion, and connectedness; the ethics of justice relies on logic, reason, and detachment. The minimal argument of feminists ethics is that *an ethics of care is necessary for a balanced moral point of view*. In short, the ethics of justice is criticized for being too unbending, uncaring, unsympathetic and too rule, principle, and contract oriented.

7. Problems with Feminist Ethics

It is true that Western culture has customarily placed men in public and women in private spheres, and it is also true that the public arena accentuates contracts, regulations, and the like much more so than does home and hearth. However, these facts by themselves do not show there is a male or female ethic; instead, it may be that the public and private arenas demand different ethics *regardless* of which sex operates in them. Women in the public or men in the private domain may have to adjust their "ethics" accordingly. It may be that an ethics of justice is as necessary in the public realm as an ethics of care is in the private world. Thus, simply because a particular ethics may be fitting to particular arenas that men and women have traditionally occupied does not show that ethical approaches are determined by sex; they may be determined by situation.

Another difficulty is that an ethics of care exposes an individual to becoming a "sucker." If the public world necessitates skepticism and self-preservation while the private world requires trust and self-sacrifice, then an ethics of care may simply be *inappropriate to the public domain*. In fact, there is a reason why rules, laws and contracts govern public reality--*we don't trust strangers*! It may be praiseworthy to have care and concern for the stranger who knocks on our door, the sales-person who sell us our car, or the lawyer who draws up a contract. *But it might also be naive!*

Certainly, we could claim that such naiveté is admirable and that we will bring our care and concern to the public realm. But most of us are not inclined to be so "unconditionally cooperative." In fact, we can advance a powerful argument that naive individuals create many societal problems, since they provide the fertile territory for the self-serving to exploit. In order to survive in the public world, our care and concern must be mitigated. If a care ethics encourages self-sacrifice in the public world few, including most feminists, would advocate it.

The reason a care ethics may fail in the public domain is that there we do not interact with people often enough, or know them well enough to be particularly caring and cooperative. In the world of our most intimate family and friends innocence, trust, credulity, and cooperation are appropriate. We trust that our parents, children, or spouses won't kill us while we sleep. (Although they might!) *Faith and trust generally, though not exclusively, apply to the private world; doubt and suspicion generally, though not exclusively, apply to the public arena.*

In addition, many question whether there is a "women's way of knowing" that differs substantially from a "man's" way. In the first place, the idea that there is a uniquely woman's way to know is reminiscent of old sexual stereotypes. According to the traditional stereotypes, men are analytical, logical, and rational whereas women are intuitive, illogical, and irrational. But aren't the supporters of feminist epistemology just reinforcing these stereotypes? Also, if there is a woman's epistemology is there also an African-American epistemology or a Catholic epistemology? However, if there is a distinctive women's way of knowing, then our previous argument--that differences in ethical values result not from sex but from situation--is mistaken. But are there distinctive female and male epistemologies which are reflected in and account for disparate kinds of moral theories?

There is some evidence which supports the idea that *individuals* learn differently. Whether *groups* of people learn and understand the world differently--have different ways of knowing and speak in distinct voices-- could be determined by careful, meticulous, and painstaking analysis. However, to the best of our knowledge no such analysis has been completed. It may be that learning style differs more by culture, socio-economic background, individual style, or something other than sex. Thus, at present no definitive evidence supports the hypothesis that women "know" differently than men.

Of course, no one denies there are differences between men and women; even their brains are somewhat different! But there are a great many similarities between the sexes too. They both love, live, and die and both possess the abilities to read, discuss, think, reflect, reason, and intuit. Quite possibly the similarities are more significant than the differences. As the noted epistemologist Susan Haack puts it: "I am not convinced that there are any distinctively female `ways of knowing.' All any human being has to go on, in figuring out how things are, is his or her sensory and introspective experience, and the explanatory theorizing he or she devises to accommodate it." We may find that the sexes differ substantially in how they know and what they value. But, at present there is no conclusive evidence that this is the case.

8. Moral Defectives

Another contemporary approach to morality comes from a group of individuals, most notably psychologists, who argue that anyone who does not accept some basic moral principles is **morally defective**. The compulsive egoist, the career criminal, the psychopath, and the serial killer exemplify *extreme* moral defectives. We can give them reasons to be moral, but they will not likely accept them because they have no ethical values. Jean Piaget (1896-1980), who spent an entire lifetime studying children, observed that most children develop through a progression of moral stages culminating in a mature ethic. According to this theory, those who do not are not fully developed.

Another psychologist, Lawrence Kohlberg (1927-1987), advanced a detailed sketch of six stages of moral development. In the first stage children believe morality is a matter of obeying authority and avoiding punishment--power makes right. In the second stage the idea of making deals becomes known--the right is self-interested. In the third stage the development moves to consideration of virtue, character, and pleasing others--the right thing is to help and care. The fourth stage is marked by the duty to laws, rules, and principles--the right is to keep law and order. In the fifth stage morality is a matter of contracts, rights, and fairness--the right is the social contract. The sixth or highest stage of morality is based upon universal principles that apply to everyone independent of rewards, rules, contracts, and so on--the right is embodied in universal principles.

In all of Kohlberg's stages there is some level of moral development. But it easy to imagine an individual at some "pre-developmental" stage. Such individuals do not have any developed moral sense. Unlike most of us, they do not shun administering gratuitous violence to others, in fact, they might enjoy it! There is simply something wrong with them. Maybe they have a chemical imbalance or were abused as children. In such cases they need chemical treatment or behavior modification, not moral philosophy. (Notice the subtle shift from the moral domain to the medical or psychological sphere.) Concerning defectives our options are limited; we can live with them, incarcerate them, alter them, or dispose of them.

In general, society has incarcerated defectives because they are averse to living with them, unable to alter them and, except for rare instances in which capital punishment is imposed, unwilling to dispose of them. If incarceration becomes too costly, time-consuming, or unpopular and we still don't want to live with them, then one of the other two options must be chosen. (Incarceration is not a good treatment for the defective anyway, since it ignores rather than treats the defect.) The preferred method would be some type of physiological and/or psychological treatment. If such treatments and techniques were reliable--if we could truly remedy the defect--then alteration may be the preferred choice. If these methods prove unreliable or unpopular, then disposal would be the only remaining option.

9. Problems with Psychologizing

There are at least two difficulties with the idea of defectives, one specific and one general. First, there is a specific difficulty with Kohlberg's theory. While the development from stage one through four is not problematic-- since it involves little more than coming to accept conventional morality-- the transition to stages five and six is troubling. After the fourth stage, individuals often raise questions about morality and may become egoists, contractarians, utilitarians, and so on. Kohlberg provides no evidence whatsoever that his fifth stage is better or his sixth stage is morally best. He simply believes they are. Thus, he acts as philosopher rather than a psychologist when he offers this pronouncement.

There is a more general problem with the idea that we can identify defectives. The cases we have mentioned--serial killers, psychopaths, and the like--are relatively non-controversial. But most cases are more problematic. What of children who steal from the drug store or individuals who cheats on their income tax? What of homosexuals or prostitutes? What of egoists or relativists? Are these individuals defective? What criteria determine defectiveness? What is to be done with defectives? Ultimately, the idea of moral defective appears to rest on some other moral principles or values which we happen to accept. If it does, it is more of a moral than clinical definition and would need to be supported by philosophical justification. But if that is the case, the idea of a moral defective collapses back into philosophical analysis.

We have now considered all of the classical moral theories in detail and have briefly touched upon the role that rights, virtues, sex, and psychology play in moral theorizing. There remains one final fact about all human beings that applies to their bodies, their minds, and their behaviors. This fact is **evolution**.

Chapter 9

Evolution and Ethics

"[Humans] in [their] arrogance think [themselves] a great work worthy the interposition of a deity. More humble and I think truer to consider [themselves] created from animals."
Charles Darwin

1. Darwin and Evolution

Charles Darwin (1809-1882) was born into a wealthy and loving English family. Darwin's father was a physician who assumed his son would follow him into the profession, but Darwin, squeamish at the sight of blood, decided to go to Cambridge and study for the clergy. After graduation, Darwin, who had always loved nature and was especially good in science, was offered a job as the naturalist aboard the H.M.S. *Beagle*, a ship that was to circumnavigate the globe. It was not that Darwin was a naturalist of any repute but rather that the captain, who could not socialize on the journey with his crew, thought Darwin amicable company. So Darwin delayed his entry into the clergy and embarked upon a trip that would last five years, provide few comforts, and for which he had to pay his own expenses. No wonder two others before him had turned down the position! But Darwin's journey changed the world.

When Darwin began his journey in 1831, almost everyone assumed that the world was: 1) about six thousand years old; 2) pretty much the same then as it had always been; and 3) designed by an omnipotent Creator. Darwin's journey challenged these hypotheses. Still, the time was ripe for Darwin. Evolution had been discussed for nearly one hundred years-- including by his grandfather Erasmus Darwin--and the fossil evidence was already causing quite a stir due most notably to the work of the geologist Sir Charles Lyell (1797-1875). Moreover, Alfred Wallace (1823-1913) would shortly arrive at the same conclusions *independently* of Darwin. Therefore, Darwin's discovery was not made in a vacuum. Contrary to what many people think, his theory is not based primarily on fossil evidence, although he did record hundreds of pages of evidence, including fossil evidence, to support his theory. Instead, the theory is based upon an argument which contains four basic facts and two inferences from those facts. We begin with the briefest sketch of the conceptual skeleton of Darwin's theory in *The Origin of Species*.

The first two facts come from population ecology: 1) all species have great potential fertility, that is, their populations will increase exponentially if all that are born survive; and 2) natural resources are limited. Indebted to his reading of Thomas Malthus' *An Essay on the Principle of Population*, Darwin inferred that in nature there is a fierce *struggle for existence* since the natural resources cannot support all individuals that are born. He now combined this inference with two facts from genetics: 1) individuals display *variation*; in other words, they are not exactly alike; and 2) these variations are *inherited*. From these facts Darwin inferred that in the struggle for existence some individuals will live longer and pass their hereditary constitution on to future generations. This process is called *natural selection*. The result of natural selection is either extinction or divergence in character traits--i.e., evolution. To summarize: *variation + inheritance + struggle for existence + natural selection = extinction or gradual change of species.*

Like any English gentleman of the nineteenth century, Darwin observed that animals were bred to produce other animals of different types. "Artificial" selection, he acknowledged, provided the model for his version of "natural" selection. Darwin knew that variations were inherited--that big horses produce other big horses--but he did not know the process by which hereditary information was transmitted. They key to unlocking this secret was the science of genetics. After his death, a copy of Father Gregor Mendel's experiments with "peas" was found among Darwin's personal effects. (Mendel's experiments first demonstrated the basic way that genetic material is transmitted.) As it turned out, the science crucial to fully understanding evolution was in a book on the shelf in his library! But it was left to future generations to forge the connection between the two.

The modern theory of evolution resulted from one of the great scientific achievements in human history, the Neo-Darwinian synthesis of the 1930s, which combined Darwin's theory with Mendelian genetics. Today, evolution--the idea that we share a common ancestry with non-human animals--finds support from a broad spectrum of the sciences including: embryology, molecular biology, geology, chemistry, genetics, population ecology, and comparative anatomy. Without evolution there is no biology; it is *the framework theory of modern biology*! Although questions remain as to precisely *how* evolution takes place, *that* it takes place is accepted by virtually all scientists as "beyond a reasonable doubt." For all practical purposes, evolution is not a theory but a fact.

2. Evolution and Ethics

Now how is evolution relevant for ethics? For one thing, any adequate theory of human nature must take into account our evolutionary origins. And, as we have seen, a conception of human nature is important for ethics. In fact, a case could be made that all of the theories we have investigated differ precisely because they operate with distinct anthropologies.

For instance, natural law theorists claim that our nature is intrinsically good. Other theories presume variously that we are: self-interested; rational; sympathetic; radically free; distinct nature male and female, and so on. In each case these divergent theories of human nature lend to the disparity in the ethical theories themselves. Thus, *the* scientific theory that tells us about the genesis and nature of human beings--that proposes a distinct view of human nature--must be relevant to our discussion.

To understand the other basic way that evolution relates to ethics, consider the following. Darwin's theory in *The Origin of Species* applied to the evolution of the *physical anatomies* of plants and animals. In *The Descent of Man*, he extended the theory to apply to human anatomy; in other words, he drew an analogy between the evolution of physical anatomy in non-human animals and in human beings. The question is, "how far can the evolutionary analogy be extended?"

It is common, for instance, to extend the analogy to epistemology or, in other words, from human bodies to human minds. "Evolutionary epistemology" investigates the evolution of mind from lower to higher forms. It also examines the evolution of ideas and concepts which are passed to succeeding generations of conscious subjects through language and education. Many evolutionary epistemologists argue that the evolution of ideas displays striking similarities with evolutionary biology. In the cognitive environment stronger ideas survive and weaker ones perish since ideas, like organisms, can be better adapted to the environment. Evolutionary epistemology also raises questions about the direction and end, if any, of the evolution of ideas. Now, can we extend the analogy from the evolution of mind to the evolution of moral behavior?

In essence, this question leads us to **evolutionary ethics**. Evolutionary ethics is an interdisciplinary field which lies at the confluence of biology and moral philosophy and, on a grander scale, science and religion. There are a plethora of theories about the relationship between biology and ethics that fall under the rubric of evolutionary ethics. However, all theorists in the field of evolutionary ethics agree with E.O. Wilson: "[that] genetic chance and environmental necessity...made the species...remains the philosophical legacy of the last century of scientific research...It is the essential first hypothesis for any serious consideration of the human condition."

A number of interrelated questions exist in the field. For example, does it make sense to discuss moral behavior in terms of evolutionary survival? Can we derive moral values from evolutionary facts? Does our ordinary morality oppose or complement evolution? Do non-human animals exhibit ethical behavior? Perhaps the most crucial question of all is how to reconcile the self-interested, survivalist behavior characteristic of the evolutionary struggle with the other-regarding, altruistic behavior usually thought characteristic of morality? It is to this question that we now turn.

3. Social Darwinism

One of the first philosophers to take note of Darwin's ideas was his contemporary Herbert Spencer (1820-1903), who first coined the phrase "survival of the fittest." Spencer believed that the struggle for existence demanded not only competition, but sometimes cooperation and thus, to a large extent, he reconciled evolution and morality. However, American capitalists like John D. Rockefeller and Andrew Carnegie misunderstood Spencer and believed that his interpretation of Darwin actually justified cut-throat economic competition. In other words, any methods or practices which do not impede the strong's survival and the weak's elimination are justified by evolution.

Social Darwinism--the idea that the social world is governed by evolutionary laws--found its most eloquent spokesman in the Yale sociologist William Graham Sumner. Sumner agreed with the capitalists that we should let the struggle for existence continue unabated. In the ensuing struggle, the strong will succeed and the weak will fail and interference with nature's "law" may bring about unforeseen and unnatural consequences. Therefore, we should let nature take its course and not intervene.

The major difficulty with Social Darwinism is that it contradicts our ordinary moral intuitions. Amassing a huge fortune while your workers toil for long hours and live in miserable conditions is hardly anyone's idea of morality. Isn't sympathy and compassion an important part of ethics? About the same time, another English gentleman proposed that evolution and ethics--far from being compatible as the Social Darwinist's claimed-- were *radically incompatible*. He was the first great critic of evolutionary ethics.

4. T.H. Huxley: Evolution and Ethics Opposed

Thomas Henry Huxley (1825-1895), a member of one of the most famous families in England, was a contemporary of Darwin and his most ardent supporter. Huxley publicly defended Darwin in a series of lectures and debates of which the most famous was the celebrated encounter in the summer of 1860 with Bishop Samuel Wilberforce (1805-1873), the most renowned cleric in England at the time. During the debate, Wilberforce sarcastically inquired as to whether Huxley was descended from monkeys on his father's or mother's side. Huxley replied: "I would rather be the offspring of two apes than a man and afraid to face the truth." A woman in attendance is said to have fainted! Years later, in 1893 at Oxford University, Huxley delivered the Romanes Lecture, the most important philosophical lecture in the world at the time. The packed audience presumed Huxley would *defend* the view that evolution and ethics were compatible. But Huxley stunned them all!

Huxley compared *the state of nature*--nature before human beings consciously intervene; i.e., the *natural process*--with the *state of art*--nature altered by human beings; i.e., the *artificial process*. These two states are in a kind of "natural antagonism" which may be understood if we contemplate Huxley's own metaphor. Envision a piece of land in its natural state and now imagine that someone cultivates a garden on this land. Human energy transforms the land into the garden and, as soon as the gardener stops cultivating, it will return to its natural state. This illustrates the natural antagonism that exists between the human intervention that creates the state of art and the natural processes of the state of nature.

Huxley admitted that human beings are a part of the natural process, but this fact alone does not show the two are compatible. A virus, for example, is a part of us but is antagonistic to us nonetheless. Huxley believed that *natural processes always conflict with artificial ones* and he reinforced the point in another metaphor. Analogous to the way an ideal garden is brought about by combatting nature, Huxley argued that an ideal society combats our natural survivalist tendencies. The ideal society values ethical behaviors like cooperation, sympathy, and self-restraint; the state of nature values natural behaviors like competition, ruthlessness, and self-interest. Therefore, ethics demands that we oppose, not acquiesce, to nature, or, as he put it: "Let us understand, once for all, that the ethical progress of society depends, not on imitating the cosmic process, still less in running away from it, but in combatting it."

But unlike the social insects which are naturally "programmed" to be ethical, human beings must choose to overcome nature. Human *conscience* is charged with the task of restraining natural behavior and is the bond that holds human society together. However, an excess of self-restraint is also detrimental to society. If we allow the unethical to go unpunished, we are like gardeners who forget to pull the weeds! Still, for the most part, the ethical battle demands an *unnatural* self-restraint.

Huxley believed that ethical progress manifests itself in *cultural* evolution. (Cultural evolution refers to the evolution of components of culture like science, religion, and political organizations.) But he also believed that powerful natural forces, operating both within and outside of ourselves, eventually overwhelm all artificial processes. Humans will continue to oppose nature by creating and developing civilizations "until the evolution of our globe shall have entered so far upon its downward course that the cosmic process resumes its sway; and, once more, the State of Nature prevails over the surface of our planet." Thus, nature eventually reclaims all it has lost.

5. J. Huxley: Evolution and Ethics Conjoined

In 1943, exactly fifty years after his grandfather had delivered the Romanes lecture, Julian Huxley gave the address. J. Huxley, who had played an integral part in the Neo-Darwinian synthesis and was one of the world's great biologists, argued that evolution and ethics were compatible. The cosmic process, he stated, extends back into inorganic forms and forward from organic forms. *Inorganic* evolution is the slow process of the evolution of inorganic "world-stuffs." As the evolutionary process unfolds, *biological* evolution leads to self-conscious human beings who in turn promote *psycho-social* evolution. At this level education, tradition, and language expedite the evolutionary process considerably. Conscious beings are conscious of the evolutionary process itself and they create ethical imperatives and goals. (The "ought" comes from the "is".)

J. Huxley identifies individual development and social cohesion as the two basic goals of the evolutionary process. Put simply, the goal is the full development of evolutionary potentialities, especially in human beings. In other words, evolution is *orthogenetic*--progressing in a certain direction and leading to the emergence of new forms. Ethical behaviors promote this progressive march toward the goals conscious beings establish for themselves, and, thus, evolution works for the good of all of us by placing within us a natural ethical "sentiment." In vivid contrast with his grandfather, J. Huxley insists that ethical behaviors promote rather than impede the natural process of evolutionary change. J. Huxley, like Aristotle before him, believed that in nature there is *an unconscious striving toward ends*. He ended his lecture with these heartening remarks: "Thus [humans] can impose moral principles upon ever-widening areas of the cosmic process, in whose further slow unfolding [they are] now the protagonist. [They] can inject [their] ethics into the heart of evolution."

In *Religion Without Revelation*, J. Huxley identified this natural "striving" of the evolutionary process with religion because religion is also concerned with human destiny. He traces the evolution of religion to help illuminate the orthogenesis at work in the evolutionary process. The "sense of the sacred" appears initially at the psycho-social level and is interpreted in three ways: 1) the sacred as *in the phenomena* (magic, fetishism); 2) the sacred as *behind the phenomena* (transcendental spiritualism); and 3) the sacred as *in the human person* (naturalistic religion). J. Huxley advocated this third interpretation. In other words, we need a new religion and complementary ethics which recognizes that human beings are destined to be the agents of evolutionary progress. "Evolutionary biology has given us a new view," J. Huxley remarked, "impossible of attainment in any earlier age, of our human destiny. That destiny is to be the agent of the evolutionary process on this planet, the instrument for realizing new possibilities for its future." Therefore, nature strives toward its ultimate completion.

6. P. De Chardin and J. Piaget: Directed Evolution

The French Jesuit Pierre Teilhard de Chardin (1881-1955) developed an evolutionary Christianity which bears striking similarity to J. Huxley's convictions. De Chardin understood evolution as the orthogenetic progress beginning at the *alpha point* and moving toward the end point of evolution, *the omega point*. Evolution begins very slowly because it is primarily a physical process without psychical energy, but the appearance of psychical energy or consciousness expedites the evolutionary process considerably. De Chardin "Christianizes" the entire process. According to his worldview, God made matter which in turn created consciousness; God, matter, and consciousness will be united at the omega point. Essentially, the omega point is a society of hyper-persons in union of love with God. The ethical imperative is that which promotes the realization of the omega point. On the other hand, the process is so dramatically teleological that the role of individual conduct sometimes seems irrelevant.

Another thinker who made significant contributions to evolutionary theory was the Swiss thinker Jean Piaget. Even thought Piaget is most known for his theories of cognitive development in children, this research was merely the means he used to answer epistemological questions, which were his primary concern from the beginning. While most of Piaget's work investigates the evolution of *knowledge*, he also studied the development of moral knowledge in children. After years of painstaking research, Piaget concluded that all of reality--social, epistemological, and moral--is evolving in a progressive direction and that his "conception of evolution" applied to all of these realities.

In essence, he argued that all of reality tends toward *equilibrium*, a balance between the organism's proclivity to assimilate from and accommodate to the environment. For example, in the biological realm we assimilate energy from the environment in the form of food and then accommodate to what has been assimilated to reach biological equilibrium. In the epistemological sphere, we assimilate ideas or concepts from the intellectual environment and then accommodate to them to reach cognitive equilibrium. It is but a short step to assume that moral evolution proceeds by adopting the moral *behaviors* that result in moral equilibrium--a balance between the organism's behavior and the moral environment. In this process some behaviors will be selected and some rejected.

Like J. Huxley and de Chardin, Piaget believed that evolution moves fastest when consciousness--itself an adaptation--appears on the scene and chooses "behaviors." In the process, consciousness comes from nature and eventually reflects back upon nature. Thus, reality comes to know itself in the evolutionary process. But Piaget does not believe some end pulls or attracts the evolutionary process; instead, we choose its course. By the end of his life, he had concluded that behavior was "the mover of evolution."

7. E.O. Wilson: Ethics and Sociobiology

But how do we reconcile J. Huxley's and de Chardin's ethical imperative in evolution with the evolutionary facts of the struggle for survival? It is precisely at this point that **sociobiology** defends an evolutionary ethics. Sociobiology alleges *to reduce* all human social behaviors--including ethical ones--to evolutionary advantage.

The preeminent spokesman for sociobiology is the Harvard entomologist Edward O. Wilson. Wilson agrees with J. Huxley that ethics arises from the evolutionary process, but disagree that evolution is *directed or moving* toward anything. This is the great human dilemma--*there is no ultimate goal of evolution; in fact, we are not going anywhere*! It is easy to misunderstand this point and most people in fact do. To illustrate we must understand, for instance, that the protective coloration of certain moths does not happen *in order for* them to survive; nor does it happen *because* there is a the threat from predators. Rather, there are simply *random variations* in the genetic material which are then selected for or against by environmental conditions. The fact that some moths--or homo sapiens for that matter--survive and others do not is entirely *accidental*! For Wilson, as for Darwin before him, there is nothing within organisms that: 1) directs them toward any end; or 2) makes them better than other organisms.

To extend this explanation to ethics, we must demonstrate that there is some evolutionary advantage to ethical behavior, in other words, it must be shown that ethical behavior *aids survival*. But how might we do this? The first clues to this puzzle came from biological research which demonstrated that the beneficiaries of the most extreme forms of altruistic behavior in animals were individuals who share significantly in the genetic make-up of the altruist. While the survival of the individual is lowered by altruistic behavior, the survival of the group, which shares many the altruist's genes, is enhanced. This biological favoring of altruism towards one's close genetic relatives is called *kin selection*. In kin selection, "selfish" genes use individuals to preserve similar genetic material.

In addition, there exists a more general altruism that has been observed in human and non-human animals that goes beyond close genetic relatives and sometimes crosses species lines. This more general altruism is called *reciprocal altruism*, so named because it relies upon reciprocity. This sort of altruism is motivated by the individual's interest in surviving; it thus bestows an evolutionary advantage on the reciprocal altruist. The evidence to support this claim comes from the pioneering work of the biologist Robert Trivers. Warning cries in birds and human reciprocal altruism are just two examples of this phenomena. Natural selection favors the reciprocal altruist because mutually beneficial actions aid survival, and, on the other hand, non-cooperation is not adaptive because non-cooperators are excluded from cooperative advantages. In short, self-interest is often better served by cooperation than by competition. (If all-out war means you might get killed, it may be better to share the food!) Thus, ethical behavior is compatible with and arises from evolution.

Now Wilson calls altruism directed toward kin *hard-core* and altruism directed toward all others *soft-core*. Hard-core altruism has nothing to do with reciprocity and is almost exclusively directed toward our closest kin. It evolved to help the *group* survive. Soft-core altruism depends upon reciprocity and is ultimately selfish. It evolved because it helps the *individual* survive. In the social insects, as Wilson has observed, altruism is almost completely hard-core, but human beings carry soft-core altruism to the extreme by making reciprocal relationships between non-related individuals. Thus, individual self-interest is ultimately the basis of most human morality.

In fact, Wilson contends that all elaborate forms of social organization, including moral, religious, and political structures, find their basis in individual welfare. Except for actions directed toward our closest genetic relatives, almost all of our altruistic behaviors are soft. Contracts and agreements that demand reciprocity, and which make human social interaction possible, exemplify soft-core altruism. This is exactly the result predicted by the evolutionary model. Hard-core altruism (kin selection) would be directed toward those closest to our genetic material, and soft-core (reciprocal altruism) directed towards those who do not share many of our genes.

The genius of human civilization, according to Wilson, is the ease with which we make and break these soft-core relationships. We move in and out of contracts and relationships based upon naked self-interest. If our altruism were all hard-core, we would exist in a continual state of group and tribal warfare, and, if we could not easily shift our allegiances, the social rules and norms that serve our self-interest would be impossible. Buried deep in our brain is the knowledge that soft-core or reciprocal altruism is advantageous to our survival, and moral consciousness emanates from these deep reservoirs.

8. Wilson and Ruse

Recently, Wilson and Michael Ruse, one of the preeminent philosophers of biology in the world today, have advanced a modified version of Wilson's original argument. They reject any theory which asserts that nature evinces values as evolutionary change unfolds because then we are reading values into evolution that biologists assure us are not there. As Wilson and

Ruse put it: "In a purely Darwinian sense, an amoeba is as good as a person." Thus, the basis of an approach like J. Huxley's has no biological foundation.

Wilson and Ruse try to forge the connection between ethics and evolution without committing the naturalistic fallacy. They begin with two scientific premises: 1) social behavior of animals is under the control of genes; and 2) humans are animals. Since both premises have been repeatedly confirmed by scientific evidence, we are led to a distinctively human, but nonetheless biological, morality. This morality derives from the kind of kin selection described previously.

Now how exactly did nature make us moral? The clue is in our intelligence. We are hard-wired with a number of instinctive behaviors from an aversion to incest to the fear of snakes and heights. Altruism, like other hard-wired behavioral patterns, has adaptive advantages and is favored by evolution. The propensity for morality is grounded deep into our biological nature. But how are these rules that govern our behavior understood consciously? Wilson and Ruse assert that we understand them *as objective moral codes*! "Nature...has made us (via the rules) believe in a disinterested moral code, according to which we *ought* to help our fellows." But biological advantage, not God or natural laws, is the ultimate foundation of our fervent beliefs about right and wrong.

But in what sense is this approach related to the traditional concerns of philosophers to ground ethics in evolution? Wilson and Ruse fashion the connection like this. On the one hand, the human species has evolved some hard-core and mostly soft-core altruistic tendencies toward their fellow creatures. In this way, morality and evolution are compatible. On the other hand, there are no absolute foundations of ethics inasmuch as our moral beliefs are instruments which further our reproductive ends. As the authors say: "...ethics as we understand it is an illusion fobbed off on us by our genes to get us to cooperate." But if we had a different evolutionary history--say we were termites--our moral values would be very different.

Still, all of this does not lead to relativism because the "ethics game" is important to our survival. Even without objective foundations, we face social problems brought about by the technology that overwhelms our biology. They conclude that understanding biology is a first step toward solving our problems. "Seeing morality for what it is, a legacy of evolution rather than a reflection of eternal, divinely inspired verities, is part of this understanding." Therefore, ethics is reducible to biology.

9. S. Gould and F. Ayala: Critics of Sociobiology

There have been many recent critics of sociobiology. The noted paleontologist Stephen Jay Gould, quite possibly the most famous scientist in the world today, has argued that sociobiology confuses the plausible notion of biological potential with the more doubtful notion of biological determinism. It is one thing to say that our genes determine the range of our behaviors and social institutions--they would certainly be different if we could fly--but quite another to say that our genes *determine* social institutions.

Gould, an ardent defender of Darwinism, also rejects Wilson's generalization of the causes of behavior in lower animals to human beings. While human behavior is clearly biologically based and adaptive, humans have gone far beyond other species in developing a non-biological means to transmit adaptive behavior to future generations. This means that human social behaviors like morality and religion have evolved far from the reach of genetic control. In short, human culture, rather than genetic controls, determines virtually all of our social behaviors whether they are moral, religious, or scientific.

Thus, Gould believes that adaptive behaviors do not necessarily have a direct genetic base. For example, he admits that reciprocal altruism exists, but this does not necessitate a genetic coding corresponding to the behavior. Even though the *range* of our potential is limited by biology, Gould doubts that there is a genetic base to all behaviors which excludes the role cultural evolution plays in directing human actions. What evidence is there that genes control specific social behavior? Gould replies: "At the moment, the answer is none whatsoever." The major reason for doubting the entire sociobiology thesis, according to Gould, is that our large brain gives us the potential to overcome biological determinism.

Another recent critique of sociobiology is the scientist and philosopher Francisco J. Ayala, who has advanced a number of powerful arguments which sever the connection that sociobiologists make between moral norms and natural selection. First, inasmuch as moral norms differ between cultures and across time without a corresponding difference in biology, the theory that morality depends upon biology is seriously flawed. This evidence suggests that culture, not biology, plays the largest role in shaping behavior. Second, human intellectual abilities have the power to go beyond biology. For instance, we may be biologically territorial, but we can decide to forego this instinct.

Finally, Ayala distinguishes between two senses of altruism. *Biological altruism* is "defined in terms of population genetic consequences of a certain behavior." Genes may prompt these behaviors even though the fitness of the individual is diminished, but such behaviors have nothing to do with ethical norms. They are not ethical behaviors! On the other hand, intentions and motivations explain *moral altruism.* Such behaviors have nothing to do with biology but with the regard we have for others. The behaviors may look similar from the outside, but we can distinguish them by the moral agent's conscious intentions. (Reminiscent of double effect and Kant.) In brief, Ayala affirms that reciprocal altruism in non-human animals is not moral behavior anymore than we would describe social insects which die for their community as morally heroic.

In trying to explain the connection between ethics and evolution, Ayala differentiates between whether: 1) biology determines the "capacity" for ethics; and whether 2) biology determines "particular" ethical norms or principles. He answers the former in the affirmative and the latter in the negative. We are necessarily ethical, but particular norms themselves are freely chosen. The capacity for ethics is intertwined with self-consciousness, a product of biological evolution, but the norms and principles of ethics are products of cultural, not biological, evolution. Therefore, he agrees with Gould that biology shapes our potential moral behaviors but does not determine them.

Biology determines the "capacity" for ethics because of the presence in human beings of three necessary and sufficient conditions for ethical behavior which themselves derive from human consciousness. First, we anticipate the consequences of our actions because we can create mental images of unreal possibilities. Second, we make value judgments about actions, ends, objects, and behaviors which we consider valuable. Third, we choose between courses of action. Ayala does not believe that evolution favored certain ethical behaviors, but that it did provide the conditions under which human consciousness, the source of all ethics, developed.

Turning to the question of whether evolution determines "particular" moral norms, Ayala claims that any attempt to justify particular moral norms with biology commits the "naturalistic fallacy." Simply because evolution has proceeded in a particular way says nothing about whether it is right or good. Simply because bacteria have survived for millions of years and in great numbers does not mean they are more or less valuable than vertebrates. Instead, Ayala maintains, moral codes come from religious and social traditions: "The evaluation of moral codes or human acttions must take into account biological knowledge. But for deciding which moral codes should be accepted, biology alone is palpably insufficient."

10. Rachels: Evolution and Human Dignity

In his recent book, *Created From Animals: The Moral Implications of Darwinism*, the contemporary philosopher James Rachels has challenged the idea that evolution and traditional ethics can be reconciled. Like the Social Darwinists, Rachels maintains that evolution demands a rethinking of traditional ethics. But he differs radically from Social Darwinists in the moral philosophy he proposes.

Rachels argues that philosophers, as well as ordinary folk, have basically ignored the implications of Darwinism because they think it: 1) has nothing to do with fundamental moral values; or 2) completely undermines them. Rachels suggests that Darwinism does undermine traditional morality but offers to replace it with something better. It is simply inconceivable, Rachels believes, that a theory as radical as evolution would not have momentous consequences for moral theory.

Rachels' argument is long and complex but the basic argument may be summarized as follows. *First,* traditional morality places special emphasis on the unique value or dignity of human beings. Human dignity derives from either God, who created humans in God's image, or a conception of humanity as uniquely rational. *Second,* Darwin's theory undermines the idea of unique human dignity and its logical support in either God or rational uniqueness. The distinctiveness of human beings follows from a discredited metaphysics and we should now recognize that humans differ by degree, but not by kind, from non-human animals. *Third,* he replaces human dignity with moral individualism. According to moral individualism, we are entitled to no special moral consideration simply because we are human. Instead, how we should be treated depends upon our particular characteristics. *Finally,* by removing the idea of human dignity we rid ourselves of a kind of superstitious "awe" that heretofore has informed moral decision-making. This shift in our perspective will have practical consequences for moral issues like suicide, euthanasia, and the treatment of non-human animals.

The major problem with Rachels' thesis revolves around his claim that humans are *not* morally special. Despite our common heritage with non-human animals our large brain apparently distinguishes us significantly. Furthermore, Rachels needs to further explain the origin and significance of his notion of moral individualism. Upon what naturalistic or meta-physical assumptions does it rest?

11. Problems for Evolutionary Ethics

It is difficult to advance a specific critique of evolutionary ethics because evolutionary ethics is a generic name for a number of interrelated but nevertheless oftentimes contradictory theories. However, there is one general criticism of the attempt to derive moral values from facts of nature that we have previously discussed--the *naturalistic fallacy*. Just because ethical behaviors arise in nature doesn't mean we should value those behaviors.

In addition, there is another problem sometimes referred to as the *genetic fallacy*. We commit the fallacy when we confuse the origin of a belief or behavior with its justification. Our belief in witches may have originated in our religious upbringing, but that does not mean we are *justified* in that belief. Analagously, a certain type of behavior, say soft-core altruism, may have arisen because it bestowed evolutionary advantage, but that does not mean it is ethically justified. It is easy to confuse the genesis of an idea or behavior with its justification.

Thus, the critics argue, an adequate ethical theory must explain not only what we do and why, but *what we should do*. In other words, they must not only explain the nature and genesis of morality, they must *justify* it. But evolutionary ethicians have a hard time doing this. If they explain the genesis by saying that facts justify values, they commit the naturalistic fallacy. If they say that facts elicit values in an upward ethical progress, they mistakenly read purposes and ends into evolution that evolutionists assure us are not there. In short, evolution may explain the origin of morality but it cannot justify morality.

12. Theories Compared

Let us try to summarize the various views of the relationship between evolution and ethics. Every single theorist agrees that it is important to consider the relationship between evolution and morality. *T. Huxley* was the only theorist who believed that the two were incompatible. He claimed that ethical tendencies, even if they arise in evolution, oppose evolutionary trends. The *Social Darwinists* and *Rachels* believe evolutionary theory forces us to re-examine our ethical values. In other words, they argue that evolution is incompatible with our ordinary ethical views but not with the morality that they suppose follows. The Social Darwinists conclude that this re-examination results in a "survival of the fittest" morality, while Rachels believes that it results in a new kind of "moral individualism" that modifies the idea of human dignity.

All of the other theorists we have discussed agree that ordinary morality and evolution are compatible, but disagree on the *meaning* of the fact that ethics arose in the evolutionary process. The *sociobiologists* believe that morality is an evolutionary product which ultimately reduces to the self-interest of the individual or the preservation of genetic material. Thus, morality is a biological phenomena exclusively. In this respect, they agree with the Social Darwinists, but they disagree vehemently that morality entails straight out pursuit of our own interests. Morality is a kind of "enlightened" egoism that helps us survive. However, they all agree that evolution has no future purposes toward which the evolutionary process unfolds. In Wilson's language we have nowhere to go.

The remainder of our theorists all reject the sociobiologists' "reduction" of morality to biology. In their view, morality moves well beyond biology even though it began in biology. These remaining theorists all believe that biology sets the parameters in which moral conduct proliferates, but it does not *determine* particular moral behaviors. Both *Gould and Ayala* believe that cultural evolution, not biological evolution, determines the future course of the evolution of ethics. However, both are clear that this does *not* mean there is necessarily any "progress" in evolution; the evolution of moral norms from the evolutionary process is an accidental outgrowth. Like all evolutionary products it is neither necessary nor universal but *inadvertent.*

It is on this point that *J. Huxley, de Chardin, and Piaget* disagree. None of them accepts a complete evolutionary randomness. According to J. Huxley, ethics starts from evolution and then moves beyond it because teleology is at work in evolution. Human evolution moves toward the complete fulfillment of the moral imperative, the necessary, not accidental, product of a goal-oriented evolutionary process. The entire process has "religious" overtones. De Chardin interprets evolution in the light of Christianity, and Piaget believes that evolution moves in the direction of increasing equilibrium. All three believe that evolution is progressive.

Whatever conclusions you have drawn, you should realize that evolution has transformed our view of reality. The theories we have examined have all tried in one way or another to reconcile ethical behavior and evolution. They have all attempted to find the meaning of human life amidst a process of evolutionary change.

Chapter 10

Conclusion

"My third maxim was to endeavor always to conquer myself rather than fortune, and change my desires rather than the order of the world, and in general,
accustom myself to the persuasion that, except our own thoughts, there is
nothing absolutely in our power...and this single principle seemed to me sufficient to prevent me from desiring for the future anything which I could not
obtain, and thus rendered me contented...
...But I confess there is need of prolonged discipline and frequently repeated
meditation to accustom the mind to view all objects in this light; and I believe
that in this chiefly consisted the secret of the power of such philosophers as
in former times were enabled to rise superior to the influence of fortune, and,
amid suffering and poverty, enjoy a happiness which their Gods might have
envied."
　　Rene Descartes

1. What is Morality?

In the public world, I submit that moral rules are contracts or agreements
between self-interested individuals resulting from a protracted process of

bargaining and power-struggling. Evolution provides the biological foundation and explanation for this self-interested morality. The long history of cooperation began with kin selection and reciprocal altruism in non-human animals and, with the arrival of human consciousness, developed into a complex systems of social rules, contracts and agreements.

In the private world, morality is significantly more altruistic and less self-interested. It relies less on contracts and more on cooperation and sentiment. Kin selection provides the biological explanation of this behavior, but I again affirm that human consciousness has surged beyond the constraints of biology. We *can* abandon our children! Thus, within the initial parameters set by biology, conscious beings choose their own destiny.

2. What Should Morality Be?

This is perhaps the most difficult question for a fallibilist. My best *guess* is that morality should consist of the rules, prescriptions, actions, methods, behaviors, sentiments, and choices that promote human flourishing, since the idea of human flourishing is consistent with both biological advantage and moral intuitions. But I do not claim to have advanced an "air-tight" case for this view, and fallible intuitions should be continually reappraised. Maybe it is better, as Ludwig Wittgenstein (1889-1951) suggested, to remain silent about what we do not know.

3. Why Be Moral?

Various theories tell us to do the self-interested, the rational, the natural, what promotes human flourishing, and so on. But all theories fail because, as the existentialists so perceptively recognized, they *explain,* but do not *justify,* morality. They cannot command our assent. Despite the efforts of Plato, Aristotle, Aquinas, Hobbes, Locke, Kant, Mill, and others, there is no totally convincing *reason* to be moral. Hume was right; concerning morality, reason serves the passions. If there were universal reasons to be moral, almost all of us would recognize and be governed by them. But we all do not recognize a universal morality and--though philosophers of ethics are prone to think this is because we don't look hard enough--there is a another plausible reason why this might be so. Maybe ultimate reasons do not exist!

To understand the way that theory does not justify moral action, consider the following. Although *we* have a reason to be moral--it benefits all of us--*I* have no reason to be moral because I can sometimes gain from immorality. If I want to steal books and won't get caught doing so, I do better if I steal them. In the *Republic*, Plato tried to show this is not so and that evildoers are burdened with "disharmonious" souls. He asked us to consider a ring that makes us invisible, thereby eliminating all of the negative consequences of immorality. Plato said that we do better if we act morally even with the ring. Most of us know better; immorality sometimes pays. *We cannot refute egoism.* But we do not have to choose to be egoists; we can simply commit ourselves to live a different kind of life. Ethics appears subjective.

4. Objectivity, Subjectivity, and the Meaning of Life

Analogous to the way we may think about value, we may conceptualize the meaning of our lives as either objective or subjective. By thinking in more general terms, in terms of the meaning of life, we may shed light upon whether morality is objective or subjective. Think about meaning. If the meaning of our lives is objective, then our lives *derive their meaning from some extrinsic source*, but if the meaning of our lives is subjective, then *we bestow meaning upon our lives*.

If the meaning of our lives is objective and independent of us, then we *discover* it. We look and search for this meaning which might be found in God, family, rationality, evolution, or pleasure. But once we find it--or it is given to us--we need only accept it. But isn't that too easy? Aren't we diminished because we cannot endow our own lives with meaning? Doesn't meaning need to be, at least partially, created?

If the meaning of our lives is subjective and dependent on us, then we *create* it. We choose to make our lives meaningful. It is a difficult and imposing task that elevates us to the state of Gods. But can we do this by ourselves? Can any kind of activity make our lives meaningful? Do we have enough control over our lives to bestow meaning upon them? Doesn't meaning need to be, at least partially, endowed.

I propose that subjective meaning is created within the parameters set by objective reality. We neither create meaning "from scratch" or just "bump into it." An ambiguous and amorphous reality provides the field in which the subject and object may be meaningfully joined. Neither subject or object takes precedence, and *reality itself is a process in which meaning emerges through the interaction of subjective consciousness and objective reality.*

Analogously, moral values emerge between conscious subjects and objects. Moral subjects without objective moral truths are forlorn. Objective moral truths without moral subjects are empty. On this view, *moral reality is a process in which moral values emerge through the interaction of consciousness and reality.* Indeed, the entire evolutionary process is one in which reality generates consciousness and in the process reality becomes self-aware. In other words, reality comes to know itself through consciousness.

But this view may be all wrong, and our lives and choices absurd. In that case, we are like Sisyphus, condemned forever to roll the rock to the top of the hill. When we finally get it there, it rolls back down where we push it back up...then the process is repeated forever.

5. What Should We Believe?

None of us know the truth. All we can do is carefully reflect, discuss with other knowledgeable individuals, and then choose. After our long search there is "no chair, no church, no philosophy." There are no moral or metaphysical propositions worthy of our exclusively rational assent, and, therefore, all of our beliefs must contain a non-rational component. In the end there are no answers...there is only hope.

At the conclusion of his Romanes lecture--the crowd hushed by the pessimistic suggestion that evolution would consume us all--Huxley expressed hope. We end, as did Huxley's lecture, with an exhortation from Alfred Lord Tennyson's *Ulysses*:

...Come my friends,
'Tis not too late to seek a newer world.
...for my purpose holds
To sail beyond the sunset, and the baths
Of all the western stars, until I die.
It may be that the gulfs will wash us down:
It may be that we shall touch the Happy Isles,
And see the great Achilles, whom we knew.
Tho' much is taken, much abides; and tho'
We are not that strength which in old days
Moved earth and heaven, that which we are,
   we are;
One equal temper of heroic hearts,
Made weak by time and fate, but strong in will
To strive, to seek, to find, and not to yield.

Bibliography

Preface

The quotation from Sextus Empiricus is from Phillip Hallie's "Classical Skepticism--A Polemical Introduction." In *Selections from the Major Writings on Scepticism, Man, & God.* Edited by Phillip Hallie, translated by Sanford Etheridge (Indianapolis: Hackett, 1985).

Walt Whitman. "Song of Myself." In *Leaves of Grass* (New York: New American Library, 1955).

Chapter 1

Lucretuis. *De Rerum Natura.* Edited by William Leonard & Stanley Smith (Madison: University of Wisconsin Press, 1968).

The description of Hypatia's death is taken from Carl Sagan's *Cosmos* (New York: Random House, 1980).

The first quotation from Bertrand Russell is from Brooke Moore's and Kenneth Bruder's *The Power of Ideas* (Mountain View, CA: Mayfield, 1990).

The quotation from Jiddu Krishnamurti is from Daniel Kolak and Raymond Martin. *The Experience of Philosophy* (Belmont, CA: Wadsworth, 1990).

The second quotation from Bertrand Russell is from his book *The Problems of Philosophy* (Oxford: Oxford University Press, 1912).

The quotation from Will Durant is from his book *The Mansions of Philosophy: A Survey of Human Life and Destiny* (New York: Simon & Schuster, 1929).

The quotation from Benedict De Spinoza is from his book *Ethics Demonstrated in the Geometric Manner* 1677.

The quotation from T.S. Eliot is taken from his poem "Little Gidding." In *T.S. Eliot: Collected Poems 1909-1962* (New York: Harcourt, Brace & World, 1970).

Chapter 2

The quotation from Benedict De Spinoza is from his *Ethics Demonstrated in the Geometric Manner* 1677.

Skinner, B.F. *Beyond Freedom and Dignity* (New York: Bantam Books, 1971).

Wilson, E.O. *On Human Nature* (Cambridge: Harvard University Press, 1978).

Chapter 3

Aquinas, Thomas. *St. Thomas Aquinas: Philosophical Texts*. Translated by Thomas Gilby (Oxford: Oxford University Press, 1960).

Aristotle. *Nichomachean Ethics*. Translated by W.D. Ross (Oxford: Oxford University Press, 1925).

Jones, W.T.. *A History of Western Philosophy* (New York: Harcourt Brace Jovanovich, 1970).

The definitions of ordinary and extraordinary means are from Paul Ramsey. *The Patient as Person* (New Haven: Yale University Press, 1970).

Chapter 4

Gauthier, David. *Morals By Agreement* (Oxford: Clarendon Press, 1986).

Harman, Gilbert. *The Nature of Morality* (Oxford: Oxford University Press, 1977).

Hobbes, Thomas. *Leviathan*. 1651.

Rawls, John. *A Theory of Justice* (Cambridge: Harvard University Press, 1971).

Chapter 5

Hume, David. *A Treatise On Human Nature* 1740.
Kant, Immanuel. *Foundations of the Metaphysics of Morals* 1785.

Chapter 6

Bentham, Jeremy. *Introduction to the Principles of Morals and Legislation* 1789.
Mill, John Stuart. *Utilitarianism* 1861.

Chapter 7

The quotation from Blaise Pascal's *Pensees*. Translated by W.F. Trotter (New York: Modern Library, 1941).
The quotation from Feodor Dostoyevsky is from his *Notes From Underground*. Translated by Andrew MacAndrew (New York: New American Library, 1961).
The quotation from Albert Camus is from his novel *The Stranger*. Translated by Stuart Gilbert (New York: Vintage Books, 1954).
The quotation from Victor Frankl is from his book *The Unheard Cry for Meaning* (New York: Simon & Schuster, 1978).
The quotations from Paul Tillich are from his book *The Courage to Be* (New Haven: Yale University Press, 1952).
Sartre, Jean-Paul. *Being and Nothingness*. Translated by Hazel Barnes (New York: Washington Square Books, 1956).
_____. *Existentialism Is a Humanism* (New York: Philosophical Library, 1947).
Beauvoir, Simone de. *The Ethics of Ambiguity*. Translated by Bernard Frechtman, (Secaucus, NJ: The Citadel Press, 1948).
Marcel, Gabriel. *The Existential Background of Human Dignity* (Cambridge: Harvard University Press, 1963).
_____. *The Philosophy of Existentialism*. Translated by Manya Harari, (New York: Philosophical Library, 1973).

Chapter 8

Gilligan, Carol. *In a Different Voice: Psychological Theory and Women's Development* (Cambridge: Harvard University Press, 1982).

Locke, John. *Two Treatises of Government* 1690.

Haack, Susan. "Knowledge and Propaganda: Reflections of an Old Feminist," *Reason Papers*, 18 (Fall 1993).

Kohlberg, Lawrence. *Psychology of Moral Development: The Nature and Validity of Moral Stages* (New York: Harper & Row, 1984).

Chapter 9

Ayala, Francisco J. "The Biological Roots of Morality," *Biology and Philosophy*, II (1987).

Darwin, Charles. *The Origin of Species* 1859.

_____. *The Descent of Man and Selection in Relation to Sex* 1871.

Gould, Stephen Jay. *Ever Since Darwin* (New York: Norton, 1977).

Huxley, Thomas Henry. T.H. Huxley's Romanes lecture is reprinted in Thomas H. Huxley's and Julian Huxley's *Touchstone for Ethics* (New York: Harper, 1947).

Huxley, Julian. Julian Huxley's Romanes lecture is reprinted in the same edition.

_____. *Religion Without Revelation* 1957.

Messerly, John G. "Piaget's Conception of Evolution." Ph.D. dissertation, St. Louis University, 1992.

Rachels, James. *Created From Animals: The Moral Implications of Darwinism* (Oxford: Oxford University Press, 1990).

Teilhard de Chardin, Pierre. *The Phenomenon of Man* 1955.

Wilson, E.O. *On Human Nature* (Cambridge: Harvard University Press, 1978).

Wilson, E.O. and Ruse, Michael. "The Evolution of Ethics," in *Philosophy of Biology*. Edited by Michael Ruse (New York: Macmillan, 1989).

The most complete source for the entire history of the interconnection between philosophy and evolution is Robert J. Richard's *Darwin And The Emergence Of Evolutionary Theories Of Mind And Behavior* (Chicago: University of Chicago Press, 1987).

Chapter 10

Descartes' third maxim is taken from *Discourse on Method* 1625.

The excerpt from Tennyson's poem was taken from *An Anthology of English Literature* (New York: Henry Holt and Company, 1931).

Index

Biographical Sketch

John G. Messerly Ph.D. is Assistant Professor at Ursuline College in Pepper Pike, Ohio. His published works have appeared in: The Encyclopedia of Multiculturalism; International Philosophical Quarterly; Kinesis; The Modern Schoolman; Philosophical Studies; The Review of Metaphysics; and Southwest Philosophy Review; among others. He has also worked as a casino dealer and professional poker player.